# The Eternal Covenant

## Mary Hajos

CHRISTIAN LITERATURE CRUSADE
Fort Washington, Pennsylvania 19034

CHRISTIAN LITERATURE CRUSADE
Fort Washington, Pennsylvania 19034

CANADA
1757 Avenue Road, Toronto, Ontario, M5M 3Y8

© Mary Hajos
First English Edition 1971

This edition 1973 by special arrangement
with the British publisher, Henry E. Walter Ltd.

*4th printing 1976*

*SBN 87508-228-9*

I dedicate my book to
H. L. Ellison
and
Juliana Ray,
old friends of mine who helped in
the translation of my manuscript

# Foreword

ONE OF THE GREATEST privileges of a traveler for the gospel's sake is that of meeting many children of God all over the world. I met Mary Hajos in Frankfurt, during a very strenuous time of work in Germany. Mary was waiting for me in a room while I had a talk with a demon-possessed woman. I looked for a partner to help me because, at such times, it is so needful to stand together with another warrior of the Lord. I asked Mary, and she immediately agreed to help. She really did help me too. We were weak in ourselves but strong in the Lord, and the woman was wonderfully liberated. I am sure the Lord is using Mary Hajos in a very special way.

This book tells of a life led by the Lord. It is the story of God's ancient people, Israel, the nation which has suffered so much and which has such an important role in world history.

Jesus lives. We believe this and experience it. Soon, when He comes, we will see Him face to face. And He will do what He has promised—make everything new. Then this world will be full of the knowledge of God, as the waters cover the bottom of the sea.

I pray that Mary Hajos' book, her ministry, and her teaching will be mightily used by God to open the eyes of His children to the important part which Israel, God's chosen people, is going to play when Jesus returns.

1971                                             CORRIE TEN BOOM

# Contents

Foreword 7

Introduction 10

PART I

1. Memories of Childhood 13

2. Searching 17

3. The Call 21

4. New Life 25

5. Persecution 29

6. Tribulation and Blessing 37

7. Portraits 41

8. An "Exodus" 49

## PART II

1. Decisions 55

2. Two Souls without Ties 61

3. The Way Is Clear 65

4. The Task 69

5. For Thy Sake We Are Being Killed All the Day Long 75

6. Praise for God's Faithfulness 85

7. The Triumphal March of God in the World 95

8. The New Song 105

   Stories from Two Worlds 113

# Introduction

IN THE EVENING of my life as the setting sun is shedding its last rays, I would like to record the mighty deeds of God as my husband and I have experienced them. Perhaps the way that leads to Him is easier to find when illuminated by the light of the testimony of a fellow human being.

This book, unpretentious in literary style, is a simple witness to those who are yearning for knowledge of the truth of God. I would like to guide my readers along our journey as God led us from death to new life. Along our way we met people, again and again, who were joining us on the road leading from darkness to light, from despair to joy, from doubt to certainty. God is faithful, and in His love desires that all should hear His voice and be led into life eternal.

MARY HAJOS

# PART I

*We were like those who dreamed.*

                                        Psalm 126:1

Chapter 1

# Memories of Childhood

ONE GLOOMY NOVEMBER MORNING when I was but a little girl of eight, the crack of a revolver shot aroused me from my sleep. My father had committed suicide in the adjoining room. The whole of my childhood was spent under the shadow of that tragedy. Many years passed before I learned the true reason for my father's action. He was a veterinary surgeon in state service, and being a Jew, was continually pestered and finally dismissed. His anti-Semitic chief had offered him the alternative of changing his religion to Roman Catholicism, which at that time was the state religion of Hungary. By denying the faith of his fathers, he could have saved his position; but being a very conscientious Jew, he chose death rather than apostasy, out of faithfulness to his God and his people.

Soon after my father's death, we went with my mother to a little town in upper Hungary where my grandmother was living, and we settled down there. My two brothers, who were a good deal older than I, studied in Budapest, and my elder sister married that year.

Grandmother's house happened to be just opposite the Lutheran church. I still remember the New Year's Eve when the maid who worked in the house took me to church. For me, this late night service was a very memorable occasion which somehow, for a short while, filled my sad childhood with warmth and light. I would

## 14 / The Eternal Covenant

have enjoyed going to this church again. Sunday after Sunday, when the bells called the people to the service, I stood at my window and gazed longingly across the street, hoping that someone would invite me to join them, but no one did.

Since my heart's subconscious longing for God was yet unfilled, I reached out my hand in the other direction. My mother had sent me to the Jewish school in our little town. Our teacher was a very serious believer of the Scriptures. We were deeply impressed by the wonderful stories of the Old Testament which he so colorfully and meaningfully enlightened for us. The story of how God led the Jews out of Egypt from slavery to freedom had a great impact on me, and raised in me an irresistible desire to take part in a real Passover feast, with all its rituals. But since neither my mother nor grandmother was a practicing Jew, they did not prepare for the Pesach. I persisted, and was finally allowed to spend this evening with a very religious family, and to take part in a true Passover feast. I can still see myself seated solemnly at the table on which lay the Passover requisites: the bitter root and the salt water, reminding one of the bitter tears shed during the years of bondage in Egypt; the unleavened bread; and a glass of wine for each of us. In compliance with the rite observed even to this day, an extra glass of wine was placed upon the table as a sign that someone else was expected. Even the door had been opened for the one who was still to come, the expected Messiah. According to the law of Haggadah, the youngest boy of the family had to put a question to the head of the household: "In what does this night differ from all other nights?" In answer to this question, the wonderful story of the Exodus was read aloud. We heard how God, in the last night of judgment, had declared death to all the firstborn of Egypt, and how all the doorposts of the houses

## Memories of Childhood / 15

of the Israelites had to be sprinkled with the blood of a lamb as a sign for the angel of death to pass by. What a joy the message of this story brought to those present around the table! Yet, I see today that this joy was only a foretaste of the joy that comes from the knowledge and experience that Jesus Christ is our true Passover Lamb!

However, for the time being, my life continued without this knowledge. Memories of my few childhood experiences in connection with God were gradually buried with the passing years. I flung myself into the life of this world, deciding to enjoy it as long as I could. Like an erring sheep without a shepherd, I had gone astray without anyone to point out the right direction. My life was already on the verge of sinking. Then a man, who later became my husband, stepped in. We met through a mutual interest in the English language. I was studying hard at that time with a view to securing an independent life for myself by giving English lessons. To improve my knowledge of English, I went to England to stay for a while.

The family with whom I lived took me to church on Sundays. I liked the simple little church with its whitewashed walls, the lovely flower arrangements, and the open Bible on the altar. I enjoyed listening to the clear words of the minister, but at that time I did not enter into any kind of relationship with the living Christ.

After some months I returned to Budapest and was soon married. My husband was from a very pious Jewish family and was a serious person, in contrast to myself. At that time I was interested only in the "present day," in making money, and in amusements. So things continued until 1938.

## Chapter 2

# Searching

> ... *In their distress they seek me.* ...

THREATENING CLOUDS now began to drift slowly from Germany toward Hungary. Signs of an approaching tempest were growing, and I was frightened out of my wits. It suddenly flashed across my mind that my being Jewish might cost me my life. This seemed all the more unfair as I was, by then, totally estranged from religious Judaism. In this state of fright I spent much time in meditation. I began to suspect some kind of connection between my mysterious attachment to God, just because I came of Jewish stock, and the blind hatred of the world toward me, which was motivated by the same fact. I wanted to escape altogether from the God of my fathers, the God of Israel. I wanted to live, whatever the cost. At that time I did not yet know that my unbelief could not alter the faithfulness of God.

One day I was struck by the idea of following the example of a number of Jews who joined some Christian Church, with the hope of escaping persecution. This seemed to me too the simplest way. If only I had the formal document, I could slip away from God completely. But as soon as I revealed my well-thought-out plan to my husband, I came up against a formidable obstacle. His plain answer was, "I would rather choose death than throw up the faith of my fathers." His refusal to follow my plan was a bitter blow, but was decisive for us both, for we were united by deep-rooted love.

In the meantime the threatening clouds over Hungary increased. Something had to be done, and I thought quick action was needed. We began to consider the idea of emigration. Since both of us spoke fairly good English and German, and since my husband also had a good command of four other languages, our livelihood abroad seemed to be secure. Our only problem concerned the future of our aged mothers. How could we provide for them after leaving the country? However, we hoped to find some solution. I wanted to find out details about possibilities for us in Britain, so I went one day to the Scottish Mission in Budapest. When I placed my trembling finger on the doorbell, I little suspected that with this step I was beginning a new chapter of my life.

A young clergyman with friendly eyes received me in his office. When I disclosed who I was and why I had come, he still remained friendly. To my amazement, my Jewish heritage even increased his attention and good will. This I could not understand, for Jews were met with contempt everywhere in those days. Much later I realized that this man had not seen me as a cowardly Jewish woman who wanted to escape her enemies by any means; instead he had seen a lost sheep that was sought by the Good Shepherd, Jesus Christ. After a long talk the clergyman, George Knight, invited me to come again, and to bring my husband with me. The next time we went together, though my husband was a little apprehensive, wondering whether the minister would attempt to convert him. To his surprise the conversation turned out to be different from what he expected. There was no other religion proclaimed but his own. George Knight spoke about the God of Abraham, Isaac, and Jacob, who is still faithful to His people. But by bit he guided us to the saving love of God, who sent the Messiah as prophesied in the Old Testament—a Messiah sent into the world as a lamb. Through His blood Jesus wrought eternal redemption.

George Knight was the first Christian ever to proclaim to us the Cross of Golgotha as the reconciliation of God with His people Israel, and the whole world. He was the first Christian who told us what the Apostle Peter said: "You are the sons of the prophets . . . God having raised up his servant sent him to you first, to bless you . . . . ." We are really amazed at what we heard.

Until then we had heard only the very opposite. It was again and again emphasized to us that the Cross meant redemption for the world, excluding us Jews. To us it brought the wrath of God, wrath still valid now in our present time, 2,000 years after the Crucifixion.

It was, for instance, in that context that my husband heard about Jesus in his early childhood. He used to have a very good friend with whom he first started school. But after the first lesson in religious instruction, the other boy was less friendly to him, and gradually became more and more estranged. Finally, after one of the Scripture lessons, the little gentile boy burst out with indignation: "You wicked Jews have murdered our dear Lord Jesus!" Completely ignorant and bewildered about all he heard, my husband, then six years old, rushed home to his mother and asked her impetuously, "Mother, when did we Jews murder a man called Jesus?"

His widowed mother, who was a very pious Jewess, sighed with tears, "Now, my little boy, so it has started for you too!" She had had the same sad experience with the four older children when they had started to attend school.

All these memories were still vivid when my husband, forty years later, now met, in the person of this Scottish minister, a Christian who did *not* withhold from him the happy message of the Cross—happy for the Jew too.

Chapter 3

# The Call

*My sheep hear my voice...*

OUR VISITS to the Reverend George Knight became more and more regular. The plans for our emigration fell into the background, and all our interests focused around the new world we discovered through his teaching. Once after a considerable time, Mr. Knight put the direct question to my husband, "Can you now acknowledge Jesus as the Son of God, and as your personal Redeemer?" My husband answered, "No, but I admire Him as the most wonderful man who has ever existed, and as the greatest prophet." "Right; then I will continue in my prayers for you," was the simple answer. From what my husband had said, it was clear to Mr. Knight that the time for full knowledge had not yet arrived for him. God's Holy Spirit had to open our eyes to our sins first, and thus awaken the desire for redemption and for Jesus, our personal Redeemer. But we thought we understood Jesus' teachings, and having felt a desire to become His disciples, we asked for baptism. The service was conducted by Mr. Knight in the chapel of the Scottish Mission. At the words of the opening hymn, "Holy, holy, holy . . ." it seemed as if the heavenly hosts were welcoming us. We were both deeply moved. I felt as if I had received an invisible white gown that obligated me to live, from that moment on, a completely different life. In the same service, which has remained a most significant experience of our lives, we reaffirmed our marriage vows within the new context. It was on the tenth anniversary of our wedding day.

Our inner joy lasted for only a short time. Soon it became quite evident that something was still missing. From the Scriptures we already knew God's holy claims, but we lacked the power to translate them into our lives.

My husband, as he testified later, fought desperately against his sins, but his will and strength failed him again and again. Finally in his despair he called upon the precious name of Jesus Christ, and then the miracle took place. At last he knew Jesus as his personal Redeemer. In body, mind, and spirit he responded to the tremendous power of God that set him free from the dominion of sin. From then onward, he had a new life. It was obvious to him that God had enlisted him for His service and called him to become a witness.

At about the same time, I too had a similar experience. Although I had not yet had a personal encounter with the Lord, the first sparks of the fire of His love were already kindled within me. While attending a service at an evangelical conference, I suddenly realized clearly that I was a lost sinner who would never be able to stand in the holy presence of God. I broke down under the weight of God's Word. At that moment the way opened for me, leading me out of death into life. In my inner self, I heard the voice of the Lord calling me to give Him my heart and my life. I prayed, "Lord, Thou hast torn the mask off my soul. I see there is nothing good in me, but I hear Thy loving call. If Thou art willing to accept me as I am, then I deliver myself into Thy hands now." While I was in tearful prayer, the bells called us into the yard where we gathered before the coming lecture. Here all of us received a Bible text daily. This morning I stretched out my shaking hand for my daily portion. I hoped to receive some kind of answer to my prayer, showing that God might accept me just as I was. When the small card was handed to me, I eagerly read the message on it: "And I will betroth you unto me for ever. . ." (Hos. 2:19). A great, holy joy overwhelmed me on that glorious sunny morning.

## Chapter 4

# New Life

> *How much more will these natural branches be grafted back into their own olive tree. . . .*

AT FIRST MY MOTHER had not objected to our belief in Jesus, but after a while she felt uneasy about it. She was disturbed because she realized that the change involved something much deeper than she had imagined. She noticed that the pattern of our lives had undergone a complete change. Many of our old friends who had shared our empty superficial pleasures gradually disappeared from our house, and with them the desire for our old way of life. It was not that we artificially changed our habits and routines. Nothing like that happened; but a new joy so filled us that there was no room left for the old false pleasures. As former friends gradually dropped away, we felt more and more drawn toward members of our new congregation. There we had found new friends whose lives had also been redeemed through the precious blood of Christ. What a joy it was to see that the wall between Jew and Gentile has been demolished, and that in the Cross of Christ these two could become truly united.

The case was different with my mother-in-law. The family thought that our conversion might shock her tremendously, and advised us to keep it all secret to spare her. She was then over eighty but still kept all the holy days, lit candles on Friday evenings, and was, in all respects, a pious Jewess who worshiped the God of Israel faithfully.

We, however, believed God's Word which said that there was no salvation except in the name of Jesus Christ. How then could we withhold from my husband's mother this most important message which had changed our lives? Naturally, my mother-in-law asked many questions after we first spoke to her about Jesus. Even today I can still see my husband and his mother bent over a huge volume of the Bible, as he unfolded for her the faithfulness of God toward His people, Israel. He explained the unbroken line that led from Abraham through Moses and the prophets to Jesus Christ. My mother-in-law became one of the first who came to know the Lord Jesus through the grace which we had obtained.

When the persecutions against the Jews reached their peak in Budapest, she was transferred from the house, already marked with a yellow star, to an emergency hospital. In spite of the permanent dangers that threatened her life, she experienced peace in Christ, and was a shining witness for the Lord everywhere. After the war we were able to take her to a hospital run by deaconesses. Here she was able to learn a lot more about her Saviour before she happily entered into His glorious presence.

Very soon afterward the Lord gave, as a special gift, the regeneration of my own mother. I did not realize for a long time that I was blocking her way because I could not really forgive her for something which had happened back in my childhood. One night before Easter, I had a desperate battle with this memory and knew that I should not go to the Lord's table the next morning unless I had removed the unseen wall that still stood between my mother and me. And Jesus gave victory! Next morning with my heart beating violently, I entered her room to ask her forgiveness, and I found the way had already been prepared by God. My mother received me with real repentance, and we met as two pardoned sinners. In this hour she accepted the Lord Jesus. Several days after her spiritual rebirth, a little girl about twelve years old visited us. She was a "completed Jew," and despite her youth, a serious believer. I could not help telling her the great news that my mother had come to believe. Then I sent the little girl into my mother's room so that they could rejoice together. They were soon deep in conversation, and passing the door I heard this little fragment of it: "Auntie, I am so glad that you now believe in our Lord Jesus, but why did you wait so long?" My mother sighed, and her voice trembled as she answered, "Yes, my child, I wish the gospel message had reached me when I was as young as you are now. How different my whole life might have been." I was really shattered by my mother's words, for her whole tragic, hopeless life suddenly appeared clearly in my mind: the suicide of my father, and the many attempts at new beginnings with resultant disappointments and breakdowns. All these could have been spared her if only someone had brought the "happy message" to her earlier.

In the meantime, more and more light streamed into our lives through the Word of God. We really experienced the promise of Jesus in John 7:17, which was one of my husband's favorite verses: "If any man's will is to do His will, he shall know whether the teaching is from God. . . ." Since we really wanted to carry out our Lord's will, His Holy Spirit revealed more and more of His wonderful mysteries to us.

## Chapter 5

# Persecution

*Let the children come unto me. . . .*

BEFORE THE SKY completely darkened over Hungary, many Jews from Slovakia found a refuge there. An old schoolmate of my husband arrived there with his family. To hide themselves, this family had to split up, so we took the eight-year-old son, Karcsi, to stay with us. At this time we still lived in our own home in a large block of apartments. We attempted to keep Karcsi's presence secret from others in the house, but we found that this was most difficult to do, especially on days when we left to attend a Bible class. One Monday afternoon when we could think of no better solution, we ran the risk of taking him along to the meeting. At this time we were still ignorant of the fact that God also calls little children and that they, too, can obtain the grace of faith. When Karcsi first heard the gospel proclaimed, his eyes shone, and he very happily joined with us in singing the lovely hymns. From then on he insisted that we should take him along whenever we went to the Bible study. He had a real desire for God's Word; I had never before met anyone who responded so spontaneously to the gospel. Karcsi was a very nervous child, excitable and fearful. This was not surprising, since he had been in unsettled circumstances for a long time. In his own country, his hiding place had been changed several times before the family had finally come to Hungary. All this had brought on a state of worried tension with which this young child had to cope. His conversion was as serious as any adult's. He was aware of his natural, sinful tendencies and weaknesses. His tears were honest, repentant tears. I cried with him as I wondered at the way God reveals Himself to young and old alike.

At that time the existence of all Jews in Hungary became even more threatened by the inventive Eichman administration. Karcsi's parents thought that the child might be safer hidden with some relatives who lived in the countryside. They hoped that no one would search for Jews there. Karcsi was in utter despair. He did not want to leave us and cried bitterly when the time came to say good-bye. We tried to comfort him, but in vain. Then, on a sudden impulse, I spoke to him about the possibility of being a witness for his Lord in his new surroundings. The thought of being a little missionary among his relatives comforted him. A happy smile broke through his tears, and after a last prayer with us he was ready to go. Into his little bundle he carefully packed his Bible.

Before these events took place, one evening after his prayers, Karcsi asked me to sit by his bedside, and he told me the most surprising thing. He spoke as if he were expressing a last will. He said: "If I have to go 'home' one day—you know where I mean—then tell my parents about the place where I am. Please, promise!" I told my husband about Karcsi's strange request so that someone else would know about it. Months later it dawned upon us that God may have given the child a premonition of his impending death. Soon after Karcsi left us, the "death trains" started rolling from Hungary toward the various German concentration camps where thousands of Jews were destroyed. The first victims were those who lived in the countryside. We soon heard that

Persecution / 31

Karcsi and his foster family had been sent to the gas chambers. I strongly believe that the child was fortified by the angels themselves until he finally met his beloved Lord and Saviour face to face. The report of their last days was brought to us after the war by Karcsi's one surviving uncle.

Karcsi's parents and his brother, all hidden in different places, miraculously survived the war. After a couple of years, I had the opportunity of meeting his father again. Then I told him, as Karcsi had made me promise, about Karci's new eternal "home."

After Karcsi left our house, the flow of events speeded up. In the summer of 1944, the air was thick with hatred that sprang from unknown depths. Until then one did not know that such disrupting forces existed in many hearts. New posters that inflamed feelings against the Jews continually appeared. These prepared the public conscience for their extermination. All men had to leave for forced-labor camps, while their families left behind were crowded together in special houses marked with the yellow star.

I, too, had to remove the name card from the door of our home and leave for a marked house where I occupied a corner of a room. The doors of the houses were locked except for the two to three hours when Jews were allowed to be in the streets. But God's Word cannot be restricted by any human measures. Jesus Christ was with us inside the house, and His sheep heard His voice. In one of the overcrowded apartments, we started regular Bible lessons. Quite a few people gathered for these occasions. While I read from the Bible or spoke about it, young Tomi, a very faithful Jew, tried hard to disturb our meetings by any possible means. With spoons, pots, and pans he made an earsplitting din that completely drowned out the sound of my voice. This was his way of protesting because his mother had become very interested in the gospel and was considering baptism. While mother and son stayed in the crowded ghetto house, the news came that the father had been beaten to death in a German forced-labor camp. The mother's mind was not changed by this tragic event; she decided to become a Christian. She made her son go with her to one of the Protestant churches where several Jews gathered for a baptismal service. Tomi later told us that he had worked himself up to such despair that he cursed his own existence, thinking that this was what he deserved for being unfaithful to the God of Israel.

When the persecutions reached their peak and the Jews were executed in masses, Tomi and his mother tried to find a hiding place. There was a tremendous need for homes where children and mothers with little ones could find a shelter. It was in November when the Good Shepherd Mission opened a couple of such hostels. My husband and I were entrusted with the care of one of these. Tomi and his mother were admitted to this hostel, together with others in desperate need. The number requiring shelter grew daily; soon we had a hundred and fifty guests.

Outside the bombs were falling, but at first we managed to maintain a relatively normal life inside the hostel. If an official had discovered that we were staying there without any mark identifying us as Jews, we would all have been killed. Around us, the Hungarian Nazi troops took their toll. Whole houses were emptied and the inhabitants were shot on the spot or driven into the icy Danube. We were surrounded by death but angels protected our hostel, and no harm befell any who were sheltered there.

In the dark cellar where we went during the air raids, the Word of God was studied by the light of one candle, even during the most dangerous hours. Tomi sat among

Persecution / 33

the other children. As the fighting approached our district, we became more and more weary from hunger, cold, and the lack of minimal comforts, but the Word of God was proclaimed daily and heard eagerly. Sometimes our one-a-day candle burned to the end before we finished our Bible studies, and in the dark cellar there was no other light except that emanating from God's Word.

On Christmas Day a very courageous Calvinist minister risked his life and came to our house. Though the bombing hardly ever stopped and troops were fighting nearby, this minister baptized many of our resident children and their mothers. Then we all received Holy Communion together. Nobody paid much attention to Tomi. No one suspected that the Lord had touched a chord in his stubborn heart. On his birthday, the thirteenth of January, 1945, he wrote in his dairy, "Today, I gave my heart to the Lord Jesus." Yes, Tomi received a new heart and a new life, and he became an outstanding witness for his Saviour. Soon after his conversion, he became one of the best co-workers in our Bible study group. With childlike simplicity but with a deep insight that came from above, he answered questions so wisely that he often surprised us mature Christians. Tomi, who had once jealously tried to disturb our Bible readings by every means possible, became a bright, shining witness for Jesus Christ.

Twenty-five years have passed. After the revolution in 1956, Tomi and his mother left Hungary and emigrated to Canada. He now lives there where he has succeeded as a mechanical engineer. He still uses every opportunity to work and testify for his Lord. He has a charming German wife and two lovely children who already know and love the Lord.

Recently he came back to Switzerland with his wife, where we had a wonderful reunion. I was giving a series of talks, and one evening they attended. In the middle of my lecture, as I was trying to explain how Jews in Hungary were converted to Jesus Christ, I spontaneously asked Tomi to speak. He gave a forceful account of his own experiences which, I am sure, left a very deep impression on all present.

Translator's Note

I spent the crucial months at the end of the year 1944, and January, 1945, with Mary and was eyewitness to all she has recounted as her personal experiences in this period. I feel, however, that the picture is incomplete and that I ought to add a few words which would reveal another side of Mary's activity during this time of persecution.

Her spiritual work went side by side with her rescue operations for people in physical danger. The Lord used her in various lifesaving tasks and equipped her with inventiveness, courage, and strength to carry them out. When anybody in need turned to Mary, her help and advice were always there, irrespective of whether the person was a friend or a complete stranger. As long as she was able to stay in her apartment, night after night it was full of people who were hiding and needed refuge.

When Mary moved into the hostel that she mentioned, she was not only the spiritual leader there but the breadwinner as well. During the most critical days of the siege, when all transport stopped and the roads were deserted, it was Mary who ventured out daily and brought back food for the one hundred and fifty hungry mouths there. This was no light load to carry on her back in a huge knapsack. It was a miracle indeed that all survived in this home. There was very severe hunger and only by

Mary's tireless excursions to remote bakeries and Red Cross depots was starvation avoided.

For her work in the spiritual realm and in physical care, all praise and glory belong to the Lord whose servant and channel she desires to remain.

Chapter 6

# Tribulation and Blessing

> *Blessed be the Lord who has not given us as prey to their teeth! We have escaped as a bird from the snare of the fowlers; the snare is broken and we have escaped!*

IN 1946, AFTER THE STORM had passed, we were finally able to fulfill our desire to travel to Britain. Our main target was Scotland. On that journey we again found that our thoughts were not the Lord's thoughts. His thoughts are always higher than ours.

For people with very limited means, a journey abroad lasting several weeks was a big undertaking. But the earth is the Lord's, and a flat purse was no obstacle to Him.

When we said farewell to our friends, we were convinced that we would return within a few weeks and that our lives would continue as before. But the Lord had other plans. We first spent a couple of weeks in London and then left for Scotland on a Saturday morning. That Sunday my husband intended to preach in one of the churches in Edinburgh. Half an hour before our speeding train arrived, my husband had a hemorrhage of the lungs. From the station, we went straight to the hospital.

God's plan was a real puzzle to us at this time. It seemed strange to us that we had been given the opportunity to travel so far, only to be turned aside. Why did my husband have to stay in the hospital with such a serious illness, in a strange city? We could not understand it.

However, sometimes God directs us into a desperate situation so as to show us more of His grace. At the time of Gideon, He reduced the number of soldiers from thirty-two thousand to three hundred to achieve a miraculous victory. A very similar thing happened to us. The Lord laid aside His well-trained, well-equipped servant on a sickbed, and called me into His service instead. Fully aware of my insufficiency, I could rely only on God.

That Sunday morning I went alone to the church and mounted the pulpit in my husband's place. I preached about the mighty deeds of God, as He had shown them in our lives by saving us so many times from danger and death. Now I knew what Paul meant when he wrote: "My strength is made perfect in weakness."

Some additional services were on my husband's schedule, but he could only pray for them, for he had to remain in bed. Our only resource at this time was prayer, and the Lord answered our prayers by helping us above all our expectations. Some good friends of ours arranged for my husband to obtain a place in a sanatorium in Davos, Switzerland, and after a few weeks he had recovered sufficiently to travel there. It appeared that I would have to leave my husband for treatment and return to Budapest. But I prayed that somehow it might be possible for me to stay with him. Even this prayer was granted. The proprietor of the sanatorium felt compassion for us in our situation, and allowed me to stay there with my husband, free of charge. In return, I was to teach English to the patients and conduct Bible studies for them. Only after a few months did we really understand why God wanted me to stay in Switzerland so long.

Reports from Hungary reached us concerning the fate of the children who had survived the war in the temporary hostels of the Good Shepherd Mission. For some there was no reunion with their parents, for they had been killed during the persecutions; others were left with a widowed mother who had to go to work. In both cases there was a tremendous need for the children to be placed in proper homes. Such homes were nonexistent except for some that belonged to Jewish organizations. Because there was no alternative, these children, who had already heard about the Lord Jesus Christ, were put into Jewish hostels. These reports awakened a great feeling of responsibility in our hearts, and we started thinking and praying about this great need. The solution seemed to be to open up a home in Budapest for those children in real physical and spiritual need. But first we had to arouse interest in the project to obtain the necessary funds.

Soon it was obvious that the Lord, who had first sent the idea, had also opened hands and hearts. Thoughts became deeds. In about six months the gates of an orphanage, located at one of the most beautiful spots in Budapest, were opened to receive the children.

However, to materialize our thoughts and prayers, the Lord first had to take me from Switzerland across the ocean to the United States. It all happened so quickly that I even had to borrow suitcases in the last minute rush. So on a glorious September day I was on the deck of the *Queen Mary,* bound for America. I traveled for about three months, even going to Canada, before returning to Europe. In Toronto, I had one of my greatest experiences. In the People's Church, headed by the world-famous pastor, Rev. Oswald J. Smith, I was inducted officially into the service of the Lord as an evangelist, with prayer and the laying on of hands. From that moment on, I knew that I had to be continuously ready for whatever calling the Lord had for me.

After my three-month journey, I returned home. By then my husband was sufficiently recovered that he could leave the sanatorium, so we both started work with great

## 40 / The Eternal Covenant

joy and thankfulness.

Years followed when we could say, "The harvest is plenteous, but the laborers are few." During the holidays, the orphanage was used for conferences for invited guests. There the gospel was proclaimed, and often there were Hungarians present who had witnessed or even participated in the Jewish persecutions. Some among them were led to repentance and conversion. We could not stop praising the Lord for His mighty deeds.

Through the years, my husband and I sowed the precious seed of the gospel. The Lord also granted us the joy of watching many of the seeds grow up to produce fruit. (I firmly believe that at the wedding of the Lamb we will meet many more whose rebirth we never witnessed. We sowed the seeds in their lives, but others watered and cultivated.) In the next chapter I want to introduce a few of those with whom we shared the gospel.

Chapter 7

# Portraits

*Repent and be baptized every one of you in the name of Jesus Christ for the forgiveness of your sins.*

MAGDALEN, DEPORTED FROM HUNGARY in one of the "death trains" to a German concentration camp, miraculously survived the war together with her little daughter, but her husband was killed. As soon as she was restored to health, she started her struggle to support herself and her child. The successful rearing of the little girl was her only aim and joy in life. A few years later, when coming home from school one day, the child was killed in a dreadful accident. As a result of this tragedy, Magdalen suffered a mental breakdown. At the same time, some other serious illnesses attacked her frail body and she had to spend several months in the hospital. During this period, she wavered between utter apathy and the desire for suicide; there was very little hope of her recovery. The visit of a young doctor, who felt a special missionary call to the Jews, started the change in her condition. With the help and encouragement given by this doctor, who first told her about the Lord Jesus, Magdalen began to show some signs of recovery. Progress was very slow, but the day came when she was able to leave the hospital and became a regular guest at our house of retreat.

\*

I first met Eva in a small town after an evening service. I used to travel quite a lot all across Hungary to give my testimony in various Protestant churches. On one such occasion, she approached me and invited me to her house. To my surprise, I found there a large number of her Jewish friends who did not want to go to the church but were eager to hear my message. It was a remarkable evening, for at that time I really became a "Jew for the Jews." Subsequently, Eva moved to Budapest where she contacted me and started to attend our Bible study group regularly.

\*

One day when I called on Eva, she happened to be out. A neighbor who saw me on her doorstep offered to give her a message. When I gave my name, she asked me to come into her apartment. She showed me into a room where a very sick woman lay in bed; it was her twin sister. They had both heard about me from Eva. Soon we were involved in an intimate conversation. Clair, the ill sister, asked me to come again and speak to her about Jesus. She was one of those "renegade Jews" who joined a Christian denomination hoping to escape extermination, but no one spoke to her about the love of Jesus. Now she had only a very short time left to find peace and reconciliation with God. During my subsequent visits, she made me talk a lot about life after death. Her physical condition deteriorated rapidly. One day she asked me to look after her sister Lilly and her brother-in-law for whose conversion she prayed regularly. When at last she died, she went to meet her Lord with joy. Lilly attended our Bible group afterwards, though her husband disapproved of her coming. On one occasion when I preached with the aid of a flannelgraph, he accompanied his wife out of curiosity. Afterwards he no longer objected to her coming, and later he joined her.

\*

At our house we had an English-speaking Bible study group which met regularly. The attendance was free, of course, while for my usual English lessons I charged a fee. Many of my pupils attended the English Bible study group as an additional conversational hour, free of charge. One of those pupils was Anna, a young mother of two. We became good friends, and she often stayed behind after the others had left and spoke to me about her problems.

She was an unhappy person who was starved for the love she had apparently never received. Her hunger for it was not satisifed by either her parents or her husband. When she started to "polish up" her English, her married life was near the breaking point. In the midst of this crisis, she discovered that she was pregnant. When she disclosed this to me, she was in utter despair. She said that her circumstances and the poor financial state of the family made it impossible to have another child. She decided to have an abortion, but her decision aroused terrible conflicts. I knew prayer would help her more than any words of advice. We prayed together then and on many other occasions. The abortion never took place.

\*

Mary was another member of the English Bible study group. She was eighteen and had just matriculated in the Jewish grammar school. Bright, pretty, and very lively—no wonder she was already engaged. Her fiancé came from a strict orthodox family. Mary was a real pest. She never stopped trying to prove that our belief was false. Sometimes I rather wished that she would discontinue coming, but no, Mary came regularly and even prepared herself in advance for each occasion. To reinforce her arguments she started reading the Old Testament regularly. George, her fiancé, came to get her occasionally, and we noticed that he arrived a bit earlier each time. By the time of their wedding, they both belonged to the Lord.

\*

My cousin Elizabeth was the pride of the family because of her exquisite beauty. Married to a very rich man, she was surrounded by luxuries, and her time was filled with entertainment and journeys abroad. In 1944, her previous way of life was completely shattered. Her only son was murdered, and her handsome house hit by a bomb. Broken and confused, she turned to the deeper meanings of life for which she had never found time before. For years we had not seen each other, but after the war we came together again and renewed our relationship. Her health was delicate and she spent much time in convalescent homes. I visited her frequently and we had good long chats. She had barely started on the road toward Jesus when she already felt some responsibility for others. She had friends she used to visit, but her own illness prevented her from going to see them. One day she asked me if I could go for her and speak to them about the gospel.

\*

When I first went to visit Elizabeth's friends, I was met by a very old lady who looked at me with rather suspicious eyes. She was Auntie Paula, and I was warned that she would be a hard nut to crack. She guided me to her daughter's room; Kate's legs were paralyzed and she was confined to a wheelchair. During our first visit, Kate told me much of her tragic life story. Her husband, a wealthy businessman, had gone bankrupt and committed suicide. Kate had tried to poison herself in her despair, but was nursed back to life. This had happened many years earlier, but she had never fully recovered. Then the paralysis of her legs made her a permanent invalid. Kate was quite eager to find out why Elizabeth had sent me to visit them, while Auntie Paula looked at me like an examiner with her bright, cynical eyes. Before I left, Kate asked me to form a little group in their house so that she could have the opportunity to meet others and to hear the gospel. At the first meeting in their home we started to sing a hymn and to my astonishment, Auntie Paula went to the piano and accompanied us. She was an excellent pianist, and though she said that she was not interested in the other part of the meetings, she quite willingly played for us at any time. My husband came with me to one of these meetings at Kate's house and had a long conversation with Auntie Paula. He spoke to her about his own mother, about her strong Jewish belief, and of her conversion. This time a spark of interest showed in Auntie Paula's eyes; the ice was broken. After her conversion, Auntie Paula's artistic talents were channeled into beautiful poetry, praising the Lord.

\*

I have deliberately interrupted these portraits at the point where the subjects honestly started seeking the Lord. They were individuals from different backgrounds and of different ages. Before the Lord drew them to Himself, their ways of life varied greatly and so did their first responses to His call. From a certain point onward until their conversion, however, their stories are so similar that there is no need to record them individually. Even so I cannot avoid some repetition, for one can observe a common pattern in the conversion of Jews.

A Jew is led to the search for deeper understanding for different reasons—persecution, personal tragedy, or simply a great devotion toward God, about whom he wants to know more. No matter what motivates the searcher, the Lord never fails to answer one who seeks. Usually the seeker meets someone at the right time through whom the Lord will guide him to fuller understanding. This human help is very necessary, though it is not by anyone's convincing logic that faith progresses. It is the Word of God, heard and read with an open heart, that does the persuading. The logic of the Scriptures, the direct connection between prophecies and fulfillments, all receive meaning with the recognition of Jesus as the Messiah. He is the "Suffering servant" whom the prophets saw in their visions, and He is the King of Glory for whom our people were then and are still waiting. Recognizing Jesus Christ as the Messiah is a tremendous discovery for a Jew, and is followed by a clear understanding of the whole Scriptures. An intensive study of the Bible usually follows as well as a strong desire to share the Good News with others. However, there are still hardships that have to be overcome.

Our Lord commanded his followers to be baptized in His name as a sign of true repentance. This was a natural act of faith for the first disciples, who were Jews. In our day, however, every Jew strongly resists baptism, even those who acknowledge the Lord Jesus. To understand this phenomenon one has to remember that for centuries baptism was an act forced upon Jews. It often meant the only escape from an inquisition or from pogroms, but it was resisted by the best of Jews, even at the cost of their lives. Baptism to a Jew meant cowardice—the exchanging of the faith of his forefathers for the religion of the persecutors.

Associated with this resistance to baptism is yet another conflict. Most Jews find it difficult to worship together with Gentiles who for generations have accused the Jews of "murdering their Saviour," and who may still be anti-Semitic in their hearts. Much prayer is needed to destroy all these emotional barriers. Final healing can only be achieved when both Jewish Christians and gentile Christians allow the love of God to destroy the wall of division between them. Since a Christian congregation is the place where unity in Jesus can best be exercised, it is essential for the converted Jew to join a church for regular worship and to take part in its various functions.

All these matters were discussed and prayed over with each of our friends before they consented to full obedience. Their baptisms accordingly became memorable occasions for other "completed Jews."

I still remember vividly the details of Anna's baptism. At this time she already had three children and the fourth one was on the way; all were baptized together. The minister based his sermon on Romans 11. Among other things, he said: "You here in the congregation perhaps think that we Christians are receiving among us a Jewish family who were 'outsiders' until now; but in fact it is quite the reverse. It is we who were branches cut out from the wild olive tree and through Jesus Christ were grafted into the cultivated olive tree of which this family was a natural branch. When we were called from among the Gentiles and became Christians, we became attached to Israel, not Israel to us!"

After the baptismal ceremony, Anna gave a very moving testimony about her faith, and the presence of God could be felt in that church. Anna later wrote in a letter what her baptism meant to her: "Standing in the midst of the congregation I felt a real and loving fellowship with all present. I came to understand how Christ, with His sacrifice for us, demolished the wall between man and man, Jew and Gentile. Then suddenly I knew I had found the love I had been yearning for, the love that neither parents, nor husband, nor even children, could ever give, the love of Jesus Christ, who died for us. Only He is able to love us in this special way. . . ."

Anna is now the mother of five grown young people, and is herself a grandmother. Her life has been one of continuous struggle, but with the Lord's help she has pulled through every difficult phase. She was, and still is, the center and strength of her family and an efficient working partner in her husband's business. Since her conversion, their marriage has been based on mutual respect and understanding, and with the passage of years their affection has grown deeper. Anna's life is a success because she can truly testify ". . . the joy of the Lord is your strength."

The friends mentioned above continue to flourish in their new life in Christ; they are forceful witnesses for the Lord, irrespective of their locations or circumstances.

Sometimes when I think of them I see a beautiful string of pearls. What a long way each pearl had to come to be a part of this lovely ornament! The fisherman had to dive deep to find the oyster, and the oyster had to die to give the pearl away. Each individual pearl is precious and beautiful; each is worthy to adorn the King.

Chapter 8

# An "Exodus"

*Some went down to the sea in ships . . . they saw the deeds of the Lord, His wondrous works in the deep.*

*For the Lord disciplines him whom he loves, and chastises every son whom he receives.*

IN THE YEAR 1953, the doctors said that my husband was suffering from leukemia, and with the burden of that illness, God led us through unknown depths.

As far back as I could remember, I had always had a terrible fear of death. Even the news of the death of just an acquaintance would cause me sleepless nights. I considered death to be a major enemy and dreaded it as such. Even after my conversion this anxiety remained. There were parts of the Bible with which I could not identify myself. The following passage found in the letter to the Philippians was one of the most disturbing ones: "For me to live is Christ, and to die is gain." I felt the first part of the verse to be very true, but my whole mind protested against the second half. When hymns containing words about our longing for our heavenly home were sung, I simply could not join in. I would have been singing a lie.

"Since therefore the children share in flesh and blood, he himself likewise partook of the same nature, that through death he might destroy him who has the power of death, that is, the devil, and deliver all those who through fear of death were subject to lifelong bondage" (Heb. 2:14, 15). This also I was unable to believe.

This was my state of mind when the doctor gave his diagnosis, and our journey through "deep waters" started. But God hides treasures in the depths. Looking back I see the anxieties and fears associated with the gruesome development of the incurable illness, but I also see the constant presence of Christ, the strength He gave us, and the peace we received. I can only say, it was all worth while. I praise the Lord for all He did in us, for us, and through us.

My husband and I were really united in great love, but there were even greater bonds between us: our common faith, our call from the Lord, and our common field of service. In these last years when every spark of human hope was gone, we realized that His grace was sufficient for us. "Though the outward man perished, yet the inward man was renewed day by day." During his illness my husband grew in faith and never ceased to proclaim the gospel with great joy and power.

Throughout the five years of his fatal illness, he never turned to God with reproach, or asked, "Why?" When he prayed about himself, he always said: "Lord, You are righteous, Your will be done." He did not seem to fight against his illness, but I tried to do it for him. I thought it would belittle God if he died of this illness, and I sent S O S letters to our friends all over the world. Individuals and groups supported him with prayer. There were short times of relief when it seemed that he might overcome the illness, and we would start hoping again. It was like traveling in a train that runs through a long tunnel. From time to time, the tunnel is interrupted by short openings where suddenly brilliant sunshine illuminates the green pastures. But, after a few seconds, the darkness swallows the train again. Twice during this period of illness, we were able to visit Switzerland. Dear friends made it possible for us to stay there, and for my husband to receive the best medical care, but the ever-growing number of white cells indicated that the disease was advancing. With some illnesses, the doctor can pretend that there is still hope for the patient, but not with leukemia. Every blood test revealed the hopelessness of it. Still I trusted that the Lord would intervene. Then when once again there was a slight improvement and I was praying with renewed hope, the Lord gave me a vision that the time for our separation had come. My beloved husband belonged first to God, and when God was ready to call him home, I no longer had any claim on his life.

These thoughts flashed into my mind when I was walking along a busy road. I did not notice the noise of the heavy traffic. Tears blinded my eyes, but I was able to praise the Lord and to thank Him for the precious thirty years He had given me with my husband. I also thanked Him for preparing me for the parting that I knew would soon come.

One evening some days later when I was just about to leave the hospital, my husband solemnly asked me, "Tell me, why do you keep on praying and fighting for my recovery? Why can't you give me back to the Lord?" All I replied was, "It has been done already." "Then all is well," he answered with a deep sigh. And after a long silence he said, "I want you to know that I go Home with joy." After that, nothing was said about it.

Then came the very last afternoon. He was lying quite still for a while, then suddenly he said to me, with a forceful, joyous voice that seemed to come from a distance. "In one hour there will be Exodus!"

And exactly one hour later, he peacefully left this "house of service" and entered his Heavenly Home.

In those minutes I had the holy experience of being completely freed from the fear of death. Christ had healed the anxiety I thought I would never overcome.

As I left the ward, and turned back to see the beloved face for the last time, my heart was filled with assurance. I knew that my husband would be where the Lord Jesus is, forever. By the time of actual parting, the worst pain of separation was already over, the bleeding wound already healed.

That is how the passing of my husband became a source of blessing to other people. When I left his ward, I had to go through a larger one where many other patients looked at me with compassion. They expected to see a broken woman, but I was able to praise God and to speak to them about the wonderful hope of eternal life. When someone leaves a dark room to enter one that is brilliantly lighted, all those left behind can have a glimpse of the light through the door that is opened. Through the "exodus" of my husband, heavenly light was seen by many still in the dark. Perhaps it was the first time that some of those fellow patients considered life after death as reality.

Very soon after this event a call came to me from the West, and I received God's definite guidance: "Go from your country and your kindred and your father's house to a land that I will show you. . . ." How could I have known then that the country to which I was to go was none other than Germany!

# PART II

*Overwhelmed by Grace*

Chapter 1

# Decisions

*Our life must be lived before it can be understood.*
Kierkegaard

ON A LATE SEPTEMBER DAY in 1959, I went out for the last time onto the terrace of our home in Budapest. The sun was up, and the geraniums around the terrace shone in luxuriant beauty. I knew that these were my last moments in my home and country. The taxi which was to take me to the station was already waiting outside the front door.

I was ready to start, but I wanted to capture everything with one last look. I did not want to forget this place which was linked with so many experiences, both joyful and painful. I was saying good-bye once and for all; I knew I would never return again. But it was not so difficult, for I had made the real parting from all I held dear long before. I began to say good-bye the moment the postman brought my emigrant's passport.

First, there were the books. Only a limited number could be taken with me, so I had to choose carefully. Which would I really need in the future? What a sorting out! Unimportant books suddenly became important; previously cherished volumes lost their attraction.

Then I had to part with many familiar things in the house, for I could take little with me. Only a few pieces of furniture and some carpets could be shipped. The choice of carpets was far from easy, for there was a story attached to each one. They were linked with memories of the hardest days of my early youth when I knotted carpets to supplement my mother's scanty pension. I had a genuine Persian carpet, which had to go with me. Its pattern on a glowing red background was exceptionally beautiful. It had always caught the eye, wherever we put it. There was a tragic story attached to it.

When the persecutions of the Jews began in Germany and spread to Hungary, one of our old friends suddenly took his life. He lived by himself and had no family; only a few friends had stood by him. He was a Jew who was well acquainted with the bloody path which his people had walked for centuries. He knew what happened when hatred of the Jews flared up. One day, when he saw disaster approaching, he sought escape through suicide. In his will he left us this very beautiful carpet, the loveliest thing in his home. That was how it had come into our hands.

Such were the memories that crossed my mind as I stood on the terrace of my home and looked around for the last time. Suddenly I remembered my parting from the congregation, and I could picture all the members vividly. It had taken place a week before my leaving, in the framework of a never-to-be-forgotten Lord's Supper. The church knew of the call that was taking me away from my old home, but no one knew the exact date of my departure.

At this service I had also been allowed to proclaim the Word there for the last time. This meeting was gloriously memorable because a Jewess was baptized. She had asked for baptism especially on this day so that it might be a kind of farewell gift. She knew what inexpressible joy it was for me when a fellow member of my people made this step in obedience to the Lord.

There was another memory that I wanted to impress firmly upon my mind in these last minutes. Our Bible study group which met twice a week had begun on this terrace. From the first fine spring day until autumn, we always met here around the coffee table. Here we enjoyed the tall leafy trees and the bright geraniums which ornamented our terrace. After coffee we used to adjourn to the large adjacent room where we gathered around the living Word. Here many had their hearts and eyes opened by the Lord through his Word and were given new life.

I looked at my watch. Only an hour remained before the departure of the train for Vienna. I tore myself away. For the last time the words over our front door spoke to me: "The Lord keep your going out and your coming in from this time forth and for evermore."

My trunks and suitcases had already passed through customs and were at the station, so I had only a little hand luggage with me. Had anyone noticed me as I talked with my minister and two of my dearest friends while I waited for the train, he would never have realized that I was leaving my homeland forever. It is strange how the minutes before a train leaves often seem strangely long—so different from the rush of everyday life. At last we heard, "Take your seats! All doors closed!" There was just time for a last handshake before the express moved out of the station.

The journey was not long because the tain made no stop before the Austrian frontier. By midday I had reached Vienna. I immediately forwarded the big suitcase with my most valuable belongings to London, which was my final destination. I wanted to spend a few months in Switzerland before proceeding to England. It was now September and by Christmas, at the latest, I expected to be in London with my godchild and his parents. They had been my neighbors in Hungary. We shared a common heritage and a common past, and we had been led through the same furnace of affliction. We had also walked together the same path of life with the Lord Jesus Christ. They were awaiting me with joy, and I was looking forward to the day when I would be with my dear old friends again. How good it is to have a warm, familiar nest where one feels absolutely at home.

I spent a few days in Vienna, and then traveled on to Switzerland, where I had been invited to stay in a holiday home run by old friends. I left Vienna about midnight, and early the next morning I was admiring the beauty of the Austrian Alps. After a long journey, the train stopped at a station where most of the passengers got out. I was glad to be alone at last in my compartment. I was beginning to make myself a little more comfortable when a man opened the door and asked: "Are you going to Germany? This is Bregenz, and in a couple of minutes the train is going on to Germany." I jumped up in fright. "No! I don't want to go to Germany—I'm going to Switzerland." "Then get off quickly. I'll help you!" In no time my bags were thrown out, and the train was moving.

"Quick! Quick! That's your train over there; it's going to Switzerland."

A friendly railway official saw me hurrying and signaled the engineer. He waited until all my luggage was on the train and left a few minutes late. I sat down in the compartment out of breath, and thanked God that I had been warned in time.

It was only a few minutes run to St. Margrethen. My destination was Speicher in the charming Canton Appenzell. There I spent some quiet, pleasant weeks.

While I was in Switzerland, I had a letter from London from a minister who was an old friend of ours. He told me that he was going to pay me a visit. He had known my husband and me for many years and was very interested in my plans for further service for Christ. We met in Zurich and had hardly started our conversation when he asked me the unexpected question: "Would you be prepared to go to Germany?" I was thunderstruck. It was like a flash of lightning on a dark night that makes everything bright for a few seconds. To Germany? This abrupt question awakened, as with a blow, much that was asleep in my subconscious. I suddenly realized that I had not yet fully conquered all the terror of the times of persecution, although fifteen years had passed since then. But the question called for an answer. Would I go to Germany? Would I live among Germans and do my service for Christ in German?

My answer burst like a cry for help from the depth of my heart: "No! never! Anywhere but Germany!"

Chapter 2

# Two Souls without Ties

I ENJOYED MY HOMEY GARRET ROOM in the holiday home in Speicher with its lovely surroundings. All around lay the soft green meadows. The Santis mountain range, though far off, seemed near enough to touch. To the west, Lake Boden greeted me with its quiet, broad stretches. The house which seemed hidden was quite suitable for secluding myself for the purpose of translating a book into English. My typewriter could be heard all day long; soon I was able to send the finished manuscript to London.

Then one night the first snow fell. The day before, the flowers in the garden had stood in their full beauty; a few hours later, they were hidden by the snow. Courageously they poked their multicolored heads through the snow blanket as though they were determined to show their wealth of color a little longer. Soon, however, winter triumphed. The rays of the sun still gave light but not much warmth. Winter had come, and I was looking forward to Christmas, which I expected to spend in London. I was soon to learn, however, that my intentions were not the same as those which the Lord Jesus had for me.

One day I went to Zürich to meet a minister who had been a true brother during my husband's last illness. We wanted to make the best use of our time before my train went back, so we sat in the station restaurant. There we had a good talk. Suddenly the minister asked me, "Does the name of Corrie ten Boom mean anything to you?"

I had never heard of her until I came to Switzerland where I had read one of her books which had deeply impressed me. When I said "Yes," the minister continued:

"Would it appeal to you to accompany Corrie on her travels around the world and to join her in her service of preaching? I am close to her, and I know that she has been praying for a fellow worker for a long time now. Perhaps you are the one. After all, like Corrie, you have no ties. But," he added reflectively, "I have no idea where Corrie may be. She flits here and there throughout the world. Perhaps she is presently at the other end of the earth. No matter. I'll write to her about you and she'll get my letter sometime, somewhere. Maybe there'll even be a chance of the two of you meeting. That would be good." We soon parted, and I took my train back to the quiet holiday home. There I went on with my preparations for a ministry still unknown to me, but I could not forget this talk about Corrie. It had awakened something that had long remained dormant.

How surprised I was to receive a letter from this Swiss minister not long afterward in which he enclosed a newspaper clipping stating that Corrie ten Boom was giving lectures in Germany and that she would be in Frankfurt for three days. He wrote that Corrie suggested using this opportunity to get to know me. I never thought that I would meet Corrie so soon or that, if I did meet her, it would be in Germany. My resentment toward Germany had to be overcome this time; I knew that these would be days of decisive importance—I had to move on.

I felt tense as the train drew into the main station at Frankfurt. My heart was beating wildly as I stepped onto the platform holding my Bible high above my head as an identifying sign. I had barely walked a couple of steps when two young men approached me. They were

## Two Souls without Ties / 63

the leading evangelists of the Frankfurt group of Youth for Christ. Corrie was the guest of this organization, and she was scheduled to speak that night under their auspices. We hurried to their center, for Corrie was waiting for me there.

We had hardly been introduced when there was a knock on the door. Would Corrie come and pray with a deeply troubled woman? She was ready to go at once, but she insisted on taking along someone who would pray with her. She looked questioningly at me, and I went with her, amazed that I had immediately been granted this fellowship with a woman who had received so much authority from God.

Corrie insisted on spending the remaining two days in Frankfurt with me. We needed to get to know each other better so that we could find the will of God. So she took me with her wherever she went. I did not know at the time that she was bringing me into contact with the living church at Frankfurt and was thus preparing the way for my future in that city and throughout Germany.

I still remember how she told me much about her life on one occasion as we were walking through the unfamiliar streets of Frankfurt. Suddenly she stopped abruptly, looked at me earnestly, and said: "Tell me, Mary, isn't the Lord Jesus blessing my work so visibly because I bless His people Israel and have stood up for the Jews?"

Deep conviction based upon the Scriptures produced a hearty "Yes." Abraham's blessing, "I will bless him who blesses you," is still fully operative.

On the day before her departure we both put our concern about our future ministry before God. Corrie had been praying for a fellow worker. Was I the one, or should she wait for another? The hour came when Corrie extended an incredibly wonderful invitation, "Come! We shall travel together throughout the world." It was an offer which opened the way for the fulfillment of my secret longing. I listened to her in silence, unable to speak, and then realized with astonishment that I had to say "No." I could not explain what had happened; I only knew for certain that the Lord was keeping me from accepting. I had to stay.

I listened to Corrie's sermon on Sunday morning, following which she had to leave for her evening engagement. There was a last greeting, a cordial handshake, and the encouraging words:

"Mary, even if you stay here and I travel on, we are linked together by the High Command." She pointed heavenward. She then left to carry the message of the ocean of God's love into the wider world. I had to remain behind—in Germany, of all places—to make known the message of God's faithfulness there.

Chapter 3

# The Way Is Clear

BEFORE I FULLY REALIZED what had happened to me, I was settled in Frankfurt. My plans to go to England seemed remote; I realized that all the obstacles which had delayed my journey to London were signs from the Lord who had different plans for me.

After Corrie left, I could no longer take advantage of her friends' hospitality, so I rented a comfortable room in a big house with pleasant surroundings.

It had gradually become clear, for reasons I could not then understand, that the doors of England were irrevocably closed to me. I became increasingly conscious that Germany and not England had been God's destination for me when I was called out of Hungary. The fact that I had had to travel to Frankfurt so suddenly to meet Corrie served as an indication from God. I did not dare to take a step on my own, so I stayed in Frankfurt.

When I looked around my neighborhood, I found that there was a large Lutheran church nearby. For some time its spire, which was visible above the houses, had served as a landmark to help me find my way home. For services I went to the church where Corrie had spoken, or friends took me with them to their meetings. Weeks passed until one Sunday morning in July I found myself irresistibly drawn to the Lutheran church which I had passed so often. I attended the early service, and I listened to the sermon with astonishment. One sentence in particular impressed me. The minister said: "If we allow ourselves the thought that the promises of God made to His people Israel are no longer valid for them, then God's promises are not valid either for us Christians." The pastor did not question God's faithfulness. When he spoke of Israel, he meant God's covenant people. He did not transfer the name to the Church, as I had heard others do previously.

I was deeply impressed with the message and wanted to have a personal talk with the minister. I phoned him and asked if I might call on him sometime. When he heard that I was a "completed Jew" he was very pleased, and urged me to come when his wife would also be at home, for she, too, had a great love for Israel. Some weeks passed before we could arrange a time when both he and his wife would be at home and free for a visit.

My first meeting with this couple was clearly marked by the Lord's presence; all three of us were blessed by our time together. We agreed to meet once a week for prayer. Normally, only the minister's wife was able to join me, for the minister was kept too busy by the demands of his exceptionally large parish. Our pleasure in common prayer increased, and the time between Fridays seemed too long. So we met twice a week, later daily, and prepared ourselves for prayer by studying the Bible together. In the course of our sharing together, we experienced something of the blessed secret of the Church about which Paul writes in Ephesians chapter two. We experienced as a reality the truth that Christ has broken down the dividing wall between Jews and Gentiles—even here in Germany.

My link with the minister's wife, Else Vömel, was a special gift of God in another way. She was the best language teacher I could have imagined. She was so eager to see me start in the service of the Lord that she spared neither time nor pains to lead me deeper into the riches of the German language. Her attentive ear missed no mistake. Even today she watches faithfully over my German.

One day my telephone rang. An unknown voice, that of an Israeli, brought me greetings from friends in Jerusalem. The speaker had come to Frankfurt to help in the preparations for the Auschwitz trial. This assignment had awakened in him detailed memories of inexpressible suffering. He, himself, had been rescued from the hell of Auschwitz "like a brand plucked from the burning." In the middle of our conversation, he suddenly asked me: "Mrs. Hajos, do you realize where you are? Do you know among whom you are living here in Germany? Did you, as a Jewess, consider all this when you came here?"

The question took me aback, but I answered spontaneously from the depths of my heart: "Yes, I know where I am living and with whom. In spite of that, or rather because of that, I am sure that I am in the right place, so I shall stay here." I realized that the Lord had been seeking, through this man's questions, my sincere approval of His leading. True, I obeyed His command when I stayed in Germany. But did I wholeheartedly approve of it now? Had my inner resistance really vanished? I knew the answer to my Israeli friend was sincere. The burden of bitter memories had disappeared; the wounds were healed. Christ Himself had made room in my heart for His love which forgives. Without this love He could never have used me here in Germany. I had been freed!

Chapter 4

# The Task

NOW IN EVERYTHING I DID, I was conscious of the Lord's preparation of me for my future service. As I look back, I can see how He did away with all my plans that did not fit in with His. This was not easy for me. To begin with, I had to learn that my ministry in Germany could not be simply a continuation of the work I had done in Hungary. There my witness was directed primarily to the many questioning Jews who had become receptive during the bitter days of persecution.

One day I had a talk with an old, experienced Swiss missionary. She looked at me thoughtfully and said suddenly: "Mary, *what* are you going to do in Germany? What is your special ministry going to be? I can't help wondering why the Saviour has led you there. But," she continued, "He will reveal His plans when His time is ripe." Soon she was proved right.

In Germany, though the first postwar years were over, the great problem still was that of coming to terms with the recent past. Else and I sought answers to many questions. After much prayer and discussion, it became clear to us that the Church bore great responsibility for what had happened. The Scriptures of the Old and New Testaments gave sufficient guidance about the will of God for Israel and the Church.

I began to get the first indications of my yet unknown assignment when Else forcefully said to me again and again: "Mary, you have no idea how much we need the witness of a Hebrew Christian in Germany at this moment. Your very presence here is proof of the unbroken faithfulness of God to His people. The Church needs you, because you are evidence that God has reached His purpose with His people, and that He will yet fulfill His whole purpose."

Yes, I felt that a completely new chapter of my life was beginning, and that my witness would be different in the future. I was convinced of another thing also. No longer would service be limited to my own people, but my new sphere of work would touch the whole Church of Jesus Christ. I would have nothing new to present —simply the whole gospel, drawn from both the Old and New Testaments and based upon the experiences and insights which Christ had given me.

The prediction of that Swiss missionary turned out to be correct. The Lord Jesus Christ revealed His plans for me, and I was amazed at the way He did it. Nothing special happened, but He enabled me to make contacts, especially with Jews, which taught me some fundamental lessons. I shall include only one instance here, but it was typical and can represent the others.

One day a woman from Israel paid me a visit. She had come to Germany, her former home, on a visit of several months duration. In the days before Hitler, when she was still a girl, she had gone to Israel as an enthusiastic Zionist. She belonged to a kibbutz with a socialistic outlook, so I took it for granted that she was uninterested in questions of faith. Therefore, I was greatly surprised when early in our conversation she referred to spiritual matters. I discovered that she was eager to know what had so gripped me, a Jewess, that I had become a Christian. There was also another question that she wanted answered: "What do you, a Jewess, tell the Christian church?"

For the time being I could answer only the first question. I told her how a minister had shown me the faithfulness and love of God to us Jews displayed throughout the whole Scriptures and how he had made it a living matter for me. I told how he had explained Peter's words to his Jewish brethren in the temple at Jerusalem: "You are the sons of the . . . covenant. . . . God, having raised up His servant Jesus, sent Him to you first to bless you. . . ." At this point she interrupted me, saying excitedly: "What did you let yourself be told? Are the death and resurrection of Jesus to mean blessing for us Jews? I never heard anything like that before! In fact, I have heard only the reverse!"

Alas, I knew only too well how true her words were. My conversation with this Israeli woman was etched upon my memory.

At that time I noticed how I was constantly confronted by the same misunderstandings about Israel's position which had obscured the gospel. Day by day, God laid these errors upon Else and me as a growing burden. I had come to know that God's wonderful saving love was still operative in the midst of His people. However, this seemed to be in direct contradiction to the teaching (proclaimed for centuries and believed so willingly) that Israel was under a curse to this day because of the death of Jesus. But had not Paul said clearly, "God was in Christ reconciling the world to Himself"? But misunderstandings had taken the heart out of the gospel and deprived it of power for far too long. Above all, the image of the faithful God who loves and seeks out the sinner had been marred.

Daily it became clearer that my work should start on the basis of this truth. But would the single voice of a "completed Jew" be heard at all? Would not my message about the faithfulness of God arouse the suspicion that I was fighting only for my people? We prayed even more urgently for God's help because we were more concerned about the Church than about Israel. It was a question of God's honor, and of His gospel for both Jews and Gentiles.

Often in my helplessness I said to Else: "I wish we were little matches which could light a big lamp." We were longing for a loud voice within the Church which would clearly express what God had specially laid on our hearts. In my despair I sent a cry for help to Professor Gollwitzer in Berlin. To our great astonishment and joy the answer came without delay: "All is well; we have already begun the work. We are going to the *Kirchentag*\* and we shall make our voices heard in the 'Jews and Christians' study group." I received this answer in the spring of 1961.

The Berlin Kirchentag really did bring us the help we needed. A rousing preparatory pamphlet showed us that the break-through which we eagerly awaited was already in preparation. The message of the pamphlet had the impact of a reformation. The errors of a number of great Church fathers, who had influenced the Church through the centuries and had promoted completely unscriptural concepts about the Jews, were clearly exposed. These errors, along with the prejudices and misunderstandings which had accumulated in the course of history, were acknowledged as grievous sins. Truly God had prepared an upheaval. That the time was ripe was shown by the manner in which the special study group for

---

\*Kirchentag is a working body of the German Protestant churches which assembles every three years for conference. It was in 1961 that Jewish guests were invited to participate for the first time. The committee called "Jews and Christians" has continued to meet regularly ever since; it has become a part of every Kirchentag.

"Christians and Jews" was established at the Kirchentag. Their work was not restricted to mere discussions of carefully selected topics; it was a genuine meeting of Christians and Jews with a frank dialogue between them.

The serious, eager way in which the majority of the ten thousand present received all that was said showed clearly that the Holy Spirit had not only given the gift of understanding to leading theologians but had also prepared many lay Christians to receive it with humility and thankfulness. Schalom Ben Chorin, the Israeli journalist and writer, acknowledged that when he entered the large hall and saw so many Christians he had asked himself what he, a Jew, was doing at a Protestant Kirchentag. Suddenly the thought came to him, "I am like Joseph; I am looking for my brothers." Many of the Christians present must have realized too that they must see a brother, an elder brother, in the Jew. This was really an about-face, which was clearly expressed in the closing session, when Professor Gollwitzer read a statement which contained the following:

"Jews and Christians are inseparably bound together. The denial of this relationship led to the hatred of Jews and to persecutions. Every form of enmity towards the Jew is atheism and leads to self-destruction. In the face of the false assertion, which has been widespread in the Church for centuries, we remember once again the statement of the apostle 'God has not rejected His people whom He foreknew.' Both Jews and Christians derive their life from God's faithfulness. The Jews are not the killers but the bringers of the Christ."

There followed an urgent appeal for the continuation of work in the home churches and all religious circles and this renewed vision. In many places this was done.

Years have passed since that Kirchentag. I have been engaged in full-time gospel work for a long time now.

I have observed how much blessing has come to the Church through the new understanding that both Jews and Christians derive their life from the faithfulness of God. What a power flows out when we put our trust in the covenant of God with Israel and with the whole world; when we accept the salvation prepared by Him and declare its validity to all.

I am repeatedly enriched by statements of different congregations saying that their changed outlook has led them to a better understanding of the Old Testament. They discover that it is a wonderful record of God's love toward sinners, of His eternal mercy and faithfulness. Indeed, this is the "good news" of the gospel. This is why Jews and Christians can join in the joyful exclamation of the prophet Micah: "WHO IS A GOD LIKE THEE?"

Chapter 5

# For Thy Sake We Are Being Killed All the Day Long*

(A sermon on Romans 8:33-39)

*Who will bring a charge against God's elect? It is God that justifies; who is it that condemns? It is Christ Jesus that died, yes, rather who rose again, who is at the right hand of God and intercedes for us. Who shall separate us from the love of Christ? Shall tribulation, or distress, or persecution, or famine, or nakedness, or peril, or sword? As it is written, "For your sake we are being killed all day long; we were considered as sheep to be slaughtered." But in all these things we are more than conquerors through Him that loved us. For I am convinced that neither death, nor life, nor angels, nor principalities, nor powers, nor things present, nor things yet to come, nor height, nor depth, nor any other thing created, shall be able to separate us from God's love which is in Christ Jesus our Lord. (Romans 8:33-39).*

IN THIS PASSAGE PAUL GIVES US a triumphant testimony to the love of God. However, it is remarkable what kindles his praise. He speaks to us of all manner of afflictions, fears, persecutions, hunger, and peril rather than of success, recognition, and security. He does not speak of those things which we regard as proofs of God's love—quite the contrary! Paul enumerates all manner of

---

*The sermons in Chapters 5 to 8 were preached in different German churches.

75

troubles to assure the young church in Rome of God's love and presence right in the midst of its problems. Israel constantly experienced afflictions, so he quotes from Psalm 44: "For thy sake we are being killed all the day long; we are regarded as sheep to be slaughtered."

In verses 35 and 36 of our text Paul is thinking of the history of Israel which illustrates this passage. How should we interpret this? How can the path of suffering be the path of the Lord?

In the burning ghetto of Warsaw, a Jew was writing his farewell letter. He had suffered terribly; his wife and five children had already been taken from him and killed. In the midst of unbelievable sufferings and fears, he wrote, as he faced death, ". . . if I had ever doubted that we Jews were still God's elect people, our unspeakable sufferings convince me that we are. No other people must suffer as much as God's people." He was right.

Can we not see that there is a link between election and suffering? If the Jewish people, even in the face of unspeakable suffering, had an unshakable certainty that their path was chosen for them by God, we must surely ask: "Where had they obtained this unheard-of faith? What was the source of their strength to endure tribulation throughout the centuries?"

There was a time in my former life when, through the rejection and hatred of others, the awareness of my Jewishness became a heavy burden. I recognized some connection between being bound to the Lord of Israel, and the hatred of the world. I envied those who were not afflicted with the name "Jew" until God gave me a new heart and opened my eyes to see in the crucified Jesus the Messiah of the Jews, the Saviour of mankind, and my personal Saviour. Only then did I understand fully the words of Jesus to His disciples, who were all Jews, that the world would hate them *because* they were chosen.

"For thy sake we are being killed all the day long; we are regarded as sheep to be slaughtered" (Rom. 8:36). The people of Israel were able to continue along their tearful, bloody path through many centuries solely because of their unshakable certainty that God was faithful. Even today the pious Jew walks his way in this certainty. Schalom Ben Chorin has written in his book, *Jonah's Answer,* which deals with the reestablishment of the State of Israel: "Jewish thought has never regarded God's promises to Abraham as a matter of history; they have always been a present reality." At all times the pious in Israel had this outlook of faith. It becomes clear throughout the history of this people how election by God brings suffering, contempt, and hatred.

The story of the twins, Esau and Jacob, reveals something of this mystery of election. We are told that before they were born Jacob was chosen. Why before he was born? Paul gives us the answer: "In order that God's purpose of election might continue, not because of works but because of His call" (Rom. 9:11). Being elected has nothing, absolutely nothing, to do with any merit or worthiness. This is not only quite strange and incomprehensible to human thought and feeling, but contradicts them. Truly, God is altogether different. God chooses "what is low and despised in the world, even things that are not" (I Cor. 1:27). Why these? "So that no flesh should boast!" The fact that Jacob was chosen before he was born excluded any possibility of self-glory on his part. He lived his life in God's light, which revealed his many sins. They were uncovered without mercy and called by their right name. We have to learn that when God elects, He does not consider human qualities.

We see, however, that God does have a basis for His choice and He reveals it to us. Deuteronomy tells us that God did not choose His people because they were more numerous than others, for they were fewer than them all. He chose them because He *loved* them. So the secret of election is love. This is the heart of the gospel: God loves sinners and elects them because of His love.

After many struggles and sufferings, God sent Jacob and his whole household to Egypt. The Lord told him that He would go with him and would make of him a great nation and that He would also bring him out again. In obedience, Jacob went down into Egypt, and God was with him. But Jacob did not live to see the fulfillment of the promise. His death was followed by four hundred years of great distress and difficulty. The family, which had grown into a nation, was oppressed and tormented unmercifully. Was this a sign that God no longer loved them and had therefore abandoned them? Quite the contrary! God was among them, and in all their afflictions He was afflicted (Isa. 63:9). God always suffers with His people.

Long before, God had told Abraham that his descendants would return to Canaan in the fourth generation (Gen. 15:16). So Jacob, when he felt death drawing near, instructed his sons to bury him with his ancestors in the land of promise. This was a wonderful testimony to his trust in the promise concerning the land of Canaan. This decision was a step of faith. For him God's promise was a reality, even if centuries had to pass before it was fulfilled. Jacob had shown his people an example of trust for all time. Joseph, too, made the children of Israel swear that when the Lord brought His people out of Egypt and back to Canaan they would take his bones with them. So sure was he that the promises of the Lord are valid forever.

If, then, Israel took the promises of God so seriously, and still does, how much more does God expect us Christians, who have the whole Word of God, to hold fast

For Thy Sake We Are Being Killed / 79

to His promises and take them seriously! Jesus is the incarnate Word of God and has confirmed all the promises given to the patriarchs (Rom. 15:8). Hence God expects both His people Israel and all Christians to demonstrate faith by holding fast to His Word. We have the great privilege of living in the time when our eyes have been turned afresh to the land of promise by the reestablishment of the State of Israel. History repeats itself. The enemies rage round about, but the Lord, who is the God of Abraham, Isaac, and Jacob, acknowledges by mighty acts of victory that Israel is His people, and so gains honor for Himself in the eyes of the world. The great privilege of the Church is to see this, and to praise God.

Now let us return to the story. When the period of suffering for Israel had run out and the hour of freedom had arrived, the Lord led His people out of slavery in Egypt "with a high hand." What followed? Were they allowed to live in peace? They had hardly left Egypt when they met the first attack of the enemy. It was from the Amalekites who did not want to let them pass through their land and so attacked them. At all times Israel was like sheep among wolves. The whole story of Jacob and his descendants is a unique illustration of Jesus' word: "The world hates you, because I have chosen you."

During the last weeks of Nazi rule in Budapest, I was able to experience in a special way what the hatred of the world can be. When the Russians were already quite near, we were still able to hide Jewish children. We gave to all those accepted false identity papers which hid the fact that they were Jews. We were afraid, however, that the male children would be examined to see if they had been circumcised.* This mark alone determined whether

---

*Circumcision for purely hygenic purposes was not practiced in Germany or Hungary. Hence this sign was the most reliable proof for the Nazis in their hunt for hidden Jews.

they dealt with a child humanely or brutally. What a proof that the attack of the Enemy was directed toward the living God Himself! This fact makes it clear before the world what kind of dark powers drive humanity, and how they rage against those who wear the mark of God's election. Hence, hatred for the Israelites—anti-Semitism—is merely hidden hatred for God.

Another proof of this hatred was the compulsory wearing of the yellow star of David. It was intended to make Jews more conspicuous during the time of persecution. Though I was already a Christian and engaged in Christian work, I had to wear it for a short time, so I am speaking from my own experience. The first time I went out of doors wearing the yellow star, I felt such waves of hatred coming from many whom I met that I could hardly bear it. Psalm 124 came alive for me: "If it had not been the Lord who was on our side, when men rose up against us, then they would have swallowed us up alive, when their anger was kindled against us."

Now let us have a short look at Esau's life. How often one hears questions which express regret that God did not elect Esau. What can we say of the life of Esau and his descendants who were not elected to be bearers of God's promise of the coming Saviour? While the house of Jacob languished in Egypt for four hundred years, Esau and his descendants were living freely and prosperously. No one seriously disturbed their peace; they were not regarded with contempt and hatred as was the house of Jacob. Why should the world hate them? They, the Edomites, were not God's elect, the bearers of blessing. *They* were like the other people. They belonged to the world, and the world loves its own. When we trace their path carefully, we can mark the point where it crosses that of the line of Jacob. It is the hour in which Herod and Jesus face one another. Herod the Edomite, a descendant of Esau, is a powerful king. In front of him stands Jesus, the descendant of Jacob. He is a prisoner condemned to death. What a meeting! The Chosen of God, the Holy One of Israel, for whose sake the house of Jacob came into existence and was wonderfully preserved over the centuries, is approaching the last stage of His path of suffering. But God said: "Jacob have I loved."

The Jew in the Warsaw ghetto, who wrote in his last letter that his indescribable sufferings had confirmed for him the election of Israel, had more to say. His letter continued: "I am dying in peace. I have been beaten but not broken; I believe in God and I love Him. . . . I die, as I have lived, in a faith in Him, founded on rock. Hear, O Israel, the Eternal is one and alone."

This unusual confession was not made by someone sitting in a solemn church service, listening to a sermon on the love of God. This confession was not made by a man who had, somehow or other, entered a state of ecstasy. It was made by a Jew, who knew that he had to expect death within the next hour. The hope that God might intervene at the last moment was completely excluded. Yet this man had the unshakable certainty that nothing—neither his suffering nor even death—could separate him from the one eternal God of Israel.

How was that possible? How was he able to trust God in the midst of his sufferings? "I am in love with God." From what source did he get his strength? Whence came the certainty of eternal life? From what well could he draw? If he had been a believing Christian, the answer would have been clear and simple. There would have been no doubt at all that he had received power and comfort from Christ. But where did he, a Jew, find such amazing power of faith?

There can be only one answer. The foundation of such a faith lies outside all human qualities and abilities. It is to be found only in the eternal *covenant,* which God made with His people and which is effective to this day. The faith of Jews is based on this covenant; strength flows to them from it, which enables them to hold on even if the way leads through the gates of death.

Martin Buber was once standing among overturned and shapeless headstones in the Jewish cemetery in Worms. He said: "Death has overwhelmed me; all the ashes, all the brokenness, all the lamentation without words is mine. But the *covenant* has never been abrogated. I might lie flat on the ground like these stones, but the covenant has not been canceled for me." For "the mountains may depart from you, but my covenant of peace shall not be removed, says the Lord, who has compassion on you."

Truly God's covenant, which He made with His people at Sinai, is valid and still in force. Buber saw this clearly, and he was right to cling to God's faithfulness and to comfort himself with it. Not only has the covenant which God made with His people at Sinai continued without interruption but it has been renewed at Golgotha. That is why Golgotha became the very place of reconciliation: "God was in Christ and reconciled the world to Himself."

If we consider God's reconciliation valid for all the world and yet exclude Israel, we negate the gospel and make God's deed of love void. The gospel which does not proclaim a joyful message for all is not the true evangel.

When Paul quoted the psalmist: "For thy sake we are being killed all the day long," he did this in the full knowledge that the gentile Christians shared the spiritual riches of Israel through faith in Christ and were, consequently, exposed to the hatred of the world in the same way as the Jews. "I chose you out of the world; therefore the world hates you," said Jesus. That was made clear to us in the time of the Third Reich, when many Christians had to walk the path of suffering too because of their confession.

Through the covenant we have not only a common path of suffering, but also a common spring of hope and joy. Both Jews and Christians are waiting for the coming of the Lord in unveiled power and glory. When the Lord comes again the path of suffering of the elect will come to an end. As Paul said in his letter to Titus, "We await our blessed hope, the appearing of the glory of our great God and Saviour, Jesus Christ" (2:13). Amen.

Chapter 6

# Praise for God's Faithfulness

> *In the sixth month the Angel Gabriel was sent from God to a city of Galilee named Nazareth, to a virgin of the house of David, betrothed to a man whose name was Joseph, and the virgin's name was Mary . . . and the Angel came to her and said: " . . . do not be afraid, Mary, for you have found favour with God. And behold, you will conceive in your womb and bear a son, and you shall call his name Jesus. He will be great and will be called the Son of the most high; and the Lord God will give to him the throne of his father David, and he will reign over the house of Jacob for ever; and of his kingdom there will be no end" (Luke 1:26–31).*

THIS ANGELIC MESSAGE was a repetition and confirmation of God's promises through the prophet Isaiah. He, too, had proclaimed that a child would be born and that the government would be upon his shoulder and there would be no end of his kingdom.

Is it not amazing that after the angelic message and later the prophetic greeting of Elizabeth, Mary bursts into praise and magnifies the unfailing faithfulness of God? Where this faithfulness is perceived and realized, there we can be sure that the Holy Spirit is at work. For faithfulness has a long past. And it is only through the Holy Spirit that we are granted glimpses into the distant past to see the mighty deeds of God and His promises. Where the Holy Spirit is at work, the focus is always on the honor and glory of the Lord. We, His Church, are also expected to join in such praise and adoration about the unfailing faithfulness of God which is manifest in His dealings with His people Israel.

This faithfulness has been demonstrated particularly in the person of Mary. Who was this girl? She was a member of the people of Israel, a Jewess from the tribe of Judah. The fourth son of Israel received the promise that from him would come the eternal King of Israel, the Ruler. David received the same promise, and Mary was a descendant of the royal house of David. To us the family tree of Joseph is better known. He also descended from David, but he became Mary's husband only after Jesus was conceived by the Holy Spirit and born of the virgin Mary. We also find Mary's family tree recorded in the Gospel of Luke, though her name is not mentioned there. It is amazing to see that while the line of Joseph is recorded only as far back as Abraham, and it leads through a son of David called Solomon, Mary is shown as a descendant of another son of David called Nathan. Her family tree is recorded as far back as Adam. This fact has a most significant reason, namely, that God made the first promise for the coming Saviour and Redeemer originally to Adam. We know well the tragic history of the fall, and the Lord's announcement to Adam and Eve of the terrible consequences of sin. At the same time, however, God shed the first bright ray of hope—the promise of the coming Saviour. He spoke about the seed of the woman, and the promise says "it will bruise the head of the serpent." The seed of the woman is not mentioned in any other passage in the Bible—always the seed of a man.

The woman whose seed is proclaimed as Redeemer is Mary. Her son has bruised the head of the serpent. The Adversary of God was defeated on Calvary. For that purpose alone was the Son of David born. In the letter to the Hebrews we read, "Since therefore the children share in flesh and blood, Jesus himself partook of the same nature, that through death he might destroy him who had the power of death . . ." (2:14). On Calvary the promised Seed of the woman brought salvation once and for all, and His victory is valid forever.

But let us return to Mary. Is it not surprising that the angel Gabriel in his message to Mary pointed to the distant future? to a future for which Israel was and still is hoping? The angel spoke of the Son of David, whose might and power will be manifest to all nations; a King who will reign over the house of Jacob forever. To this duty, to become the mother of the Prince of Glory, Mary answered an obedient Yes. What astonished her was that the angel spoke about her becoming pregnant, though she was a virgin. She expressed it this way, "How can this be, since I have no husband?" And the answer was that the child would be conceived by the Holy Spirit.

We must note that the angel Gabriel revealed only the glory of the coming King, but did not even mention that the child would become a "man of sorrows," the suffering Servant, the Lamb of God. This had to be hidden, concealed from her, and also from the people of Israel, for it was the mystery of the love of God for the world, which, according to the plan of God, was only revealed through the Apostle Paul after the finished work of redemption through the cross and the sealing of it through the resurrection.

A few days after the visit of the angel, Mary went to visit her cousin Elizabeth who lived in the mountains. Elizabeth, filled with the holy Spirit, greeted Mary as the mother of her Lord: "O blessed are you who believed that there would be a fulfillment of what was spoken to you from the Lord." With this prophetic greeting the overwhelming message of the angel was confirmed. Mary needed this reassurance; wholeheartedly she praised the unfailing faithfulness of God: "My soul magnifies the Lord, and my spirit rejoices in God my Saviour . . . He has helped His servant Israel, in remembrance of His mercy, as He spoke to our fathers, to Abraham and to his posterity for ever." Mary was convinced that the Lord would keep His promise and that the promised King would come.

Then came the hour when this child was due to be born. The prophet Micah had named even the very place where this was to happen: "But you, Bethlehem . . . though you are little among the clans of Judah, from you shall come forth unto me one who is to be ruler of Israel . . . ." When the emperor Augustus ordered that everybody had to be registered, Mary and Joseph—both of the house of David—were compelled to go to Bethlehem. But with this journey Mary started on the path of suffering. Bethlehem, like all other towns, was overcrowded with people who had to travel to their place of birth. There was no room for Mary and Joseph in an inn, and finally they settled for the night in a stable. Here the infant Jesus was born, and a manger became his first cradle. Every mother can understand what all this deprivation must have meant to Mary. But the later years of her son's life were equally hard for her. She could not understand her son, least of all on Good Friday. And as her son hung on the Roman gallows and breathed out his life on the cross, Mary was convinced that this son of hers could not have been the promised King of Israel. Let us not forget that the mystery of the incarnation and of the Cross was still veiled and hidden. No one, not a single member of the people of Israel, could have known at that time that Christ had to go through suffering into His glory. This God Himself disclosed only after

## Praise for God's Faithfulness / 89

the resurrection. But how? It was the risen Lord Himself who opened their eyes, or as it is written, "He opened their minds to understand the Scriptures," that His disciples might be able to recognize in the suffering servant the Lamb of God, the King of glory, their Messiah. This inability to understand made Good Friday even darker and more painful for Mary; not only for her, but also for the disciples. They were all Jews, still under the "veil"; that is why they expected their Messiah to come in obvious power and glory. Their hope for a glorious Messiah was kindled by the visions of the prophets and by many beautiful psalms; instead of that He died on a cross. What a painful disappointment! They were really desperate. How downcast in their hopes they were when some of them left Jerusalem on the way to Emmaus. Even when Jesus was still with them, whenever He spoke to them of His forthcoming suffering and death and resurrection they were unable to understand. Only when the risen Lord Jesus Himself came to meet His sad disciples and opened their minds were they able to recognize the crucified man to be the Lord of Glory, their God and Saviour.

And now a question: Why did the angel speak only of the glory of the coming King, and why did he not reveal anything about His suffering in the more immediate future? I believe it was the compassionate love of God toward Mary. He knew that no expectant mother could bear the thought that her child was destined to an early and terrible death. Do we ever express our special gratitude to the Lord for hiding the future from us? We are shown only the step we now have to take—the present; the morrow is graciously hidden from our eyes.

I think, for instance, about the time of the persecution in Hungary. Had we known in advance the events of the next hour—the sudden separation from loved ones who were carried off to be killed—I am sure we could not have endured. It was the Lord's grace indeed that He hid the future and gave strength from hour to hour as the need arose. Then I fully understood the words of Jesus, "Do not be anxious about tomorrow; tomorrow will look after itself. Each day has troubles enough of its own."

Only one man was ever able to live with the knowledge of His future suffering and early death, and this was Jesus. He Himself said that He came not to reign, but to serve and to offer up His life. Is it not amazing? Gabriel the angel announced Jesus as the coming King and Lord who will come to reign—and Jesus declares the very opposite!

Some years ago there was a dreadful accident in a coal mine which was reported in all the newspapers. A group of miners were trapped when part of a shaft collapsed and they found themselves cut off from life and from the possibility of ascending again to the surface. Their only hope was that someone would save them from their "imprisonment." Fortunately there were some who ventured down to help, risking their lives in the rescue operation. They took the risk—strongly hoping that no harm would come to them. This attitude is normal and human. But when Jesus left His glory and came down from heaven to us who were buried alive in our sins, He knew that His rescue operation would cost Him His life.

And now a second answer to the question why the angel had to conceal the coming of Jesus as the Lamb of God, the Man of sorrow, and was to proclaim only the coming of the Lord of Glory. This too happened through the saving love of God—not merely through His love toward Mary and her people, Israel, but to the whole world! For only through the so-called "veil," through the impossibility of recognizing in the man Jesus the promised King and Lord, could God bring salvation to the world.

And here we have the deepest glimpse into Israel's mystery: It is His saving love for us all that prompted God to call this people into being—that through them He might bring salvation to the world. Israel is the only people in the world who were not premitted to worship anybody or anything but the one true and invisible God. He Himself gave the prayer and the command to them: "Hear, O Israel, the Lord your God is the only God . . . you shall have no other gods before me." This accounts for the fact that God gave Israel a law according to which anybody who abuses the name of God should be punished by death (Lev. 24:16).

How often have I already discovered that my heart is far to narrow to grasp the love of God! I think of the words of Jesus: "So has God loved the world that He gave His only begotten Son. . . ." God gave Him. Jesus also said: "Nobody takes my life but I lay it down myself . . . such a command have I received from my Father" (John 10:18). "I came to serve and to die." God Himself ordered the sacrificial blood upon the altar to cover the sins of His people Israel (Lev. 17:11) until the time would be fulfilled and Jesus, the only true High Priest and Lamb, in one person, would come to offer Himself as an eternal sacrifice, bringing salvation not only to Israel but to the whole world.

When Jesus, a Jew, stood before the high priests and scribes and openly declared that He was the Son of the one living God, He knew that the law of Moses must be brought into operation. Nobody knew better than Jesus about the "veil" that prevented Jews from recognizing Him. It is something beyond human understanding. Here we can catch a glimpse into the depth, breadth, and height of the love of God. The giver of the law, the eternal God who came in the person of Jesus to reconcile the world, gives Himself to death by His own law!

92 / The Eternal Covenant

All this He has done to bring salvation to Israel and through Israel to the whole world. He, the promised seed of the woman, goes freely and by His own will to the cross to crush the head of the serpent through His death. Through the blood of Jesus a new and living way was opened up for the whole world. Thus we see how God gave both His law and the "veil" in order to bring salvation. So we can justly call the mystery of Israel the mystery of the saving love of God for the whole world.

And finally the third and last answer to our question, Why did the angel Gabriel announce the coming of the mighty King whose kingdom is eternal?

Dear friends, we live in a world of so many theories, ideals, even many theologies, that we forget so easily about the hope by which we Christians ought to be living. We need to be reminded again and again that the Lord *is coming.* Now is the time of the Church, the time of evangelization, when God is calling through His Word men and women of both the people of Israel and the gentile world to be the firstfruits of the new creation. The Church is the uplifted sign of the triumph of God achieved through Calvary. For it consists of such as can gladly profess: "If anyone is in Christ, he is a new creation." The message of the angel Gabriel was given to us all as a permanent reminder that the Lord, the King of Glory, will come exactly as He was announced first by the prophets and finally by Gabriel.

What power that living hope for the coming King and Messiah holds is so obvious when we look at Israel. Remember that they have been waiting more than three thousand years, and are still waiting to this day, for the coming of the promised Messiah and King. Israel and the Church are one in this wonderful expectation, in this living hope. Israel is looking for the coming of the King and Messiah, and we Christians are expecting Him who came first as the Lamb of God to return in glory.

Therefore let us join with Mary in her song of praise, in the words of the apostle, " . . . we are awaiting our blessed hope, the appearing of the glory of our great God and Saviour Jesus Christ, who gave Himself for us. . . ." Amen.

Chapter 7

# The Triumphal March of God in the World

*And Jesus, full of the Holy Spirit, came back from the Jordan and was led about by the Spirit in the wilderness for forty days while He was tempted by the devil. And He ate nothing during those days, and when they ended, He was hungry. And the devil said to Him, "If you are the Son of God, tell this stone to become bread." And Jesus replied, "It is written, 'Man shall not live by bread only, but by every word of God.'" And the devil led Him up into a mountain and showed Him all the kingdoms of the earth in a moment of time, and said to Him, "I will give You all this domain and its glory, for it has been delivered to me, to give to whomever I wish. If therefore You worship me, it shall all be Yours." Jesus answered him and said, "Get behind me, Satan, for it is written, 'You shall worship the Lord your God and serve Him alone.'" And he took Him to Jerusalem and set Him on the pinnacle of the temple and said to Him, "If You are the Son of God, throw Yourself down from here, because it is written, 'He will give His angels charge over You, to guard You,' and 'They will bear You up on their hands lest You strike Your foot against a stone.'" And Jesus replied, "It is said, 'You shall not test the Lord your God.'" And when the devil had finished every temptation, he left Him for a while. Jesus then returned to Galilee in the power of the Spirit, and His fame spread throughout the surrounding district. And He taught in their synagogues and was praised by all (Luke 4:1–15).*

*Since the children share in flesh and blood, He Himself*

96 / The Eternal Covenant

> *partook of the same nature, that through death He might destroy him who had the power of death, that is, the devil (Heb. 2:14).*

THE STORY OF JESUS' TEMPTATION is the story of a crisis. What a crisis involves and where it may lead has become known to our generation as to no previous generation. We live in a time laden with crises and are well aware that there are many things that hang on a thread. Crises involve weighty decisions, often involving life and death.

I can still remember a crisis that we Jews had to go through in Budapest. Death trains bound for Auschwitz had been rolling across the country for months. The wave of horror also reached the outskirts of Budapest. Only we who lived in the center of the capital were relatively free. But one day horrifying indications made us realize that our turn had come at last. I still recall how the consciousness of that crisis moved in on us like an icy wind of death. Our lives were at stake. The alternatives were a horrible death, or rescue. In those unforgettable days I learned what a crisis could involve.

What, however, are all the crises which men have ever experienced here on earth compared with the altogether unique crisis of Jesus and Satan facing one another as representatives of the two realities which lie behind everything: the power of life, and the power of death? Jesus and Satan: On the one hand was Jesus, the embodiment and bringer of life, the promised seed of the woman, who was to come to crush the head of the serpent; and on the other Satan, the serpent, the enemy, the one who had the power of death.

Jesus had been in the desert forty days and forty nights, where He was tempted by the devil. We are not given any details of the temptation, but when the days were ended, Jesus was hungry. Hunger hurts; it must have caused suffering to Jesus as well. Satan used this state of physical weakness for the climax of his attacks. "If you are the son of God, command this stone to become bread." But Jesus knew better. He, the "mighty one of Jacob," had to empty Himself of all might and suffer all the pain and frustration that humanity had to endure. To use power for self-gratification would have destroyed His ministry.

Jesus, the promised Saviour of the world, started on the road to the cross to lead redeemed worshipers to God. To counteract this, Satan showed Him all the riches and glory of the world. "All these I will give you if you worship me." He who emptied Himself of all power in order to carry out the work of redemption was prepared to suffer and to die. To prevent this, Satan challenged Him to demonstrate His Sonship and suggested that Jesus cast Himself down from the pinnacle of the temple. But Jesus was not enticed away from the path of obedience. He resisted all temptations, and overcame the enemy and the crisis.

What was actually at stake in those crucial moments was so tremendous that we can hardly express it in words. In the temptation of Jesus, the redemption of mankind and the restoration of the whole universe was at stake—which meant the breaking of the power of Satan as well. At all costs the tempter wanted to frustrate God's loving plan for the salvation of the world. He united all his wiles and efforts to make sure that the blood of reconciliation, the blood of the eternal Covenant, would not be shed on Calvary.

Let us follow the path of God's love for the world that eventually led to this decisive hour.

Imagine an enormous iceberg; only the peak rises above the water level. The bulk of such a mountain reaches deep and wide into the sea and remains hidden from our eyes. So it is with the depth and breadth of the love of God. Its visible manifestation is the Cross, but it has great depth and breadth which are not apparent.

The path of the saving love of God began in the depth. It began with God choosing Abram out of the sea of mankind. God promised Abraham this seed Jesus, the Saviour and Redeemer in whom all the nations should be blessed. Through Abraham and his son Isaac, and ultimately Isaac's son Jacob, God called into being a people through whom salvation was to be brought to the world—through whom Jesus was to come and lay down His life as a ransom. As the history of this people, Israel, unfolds before our eyes, we see that the same enemy who tempted Jesus had already been in action throughout history to frustrate the plan of God for the redemption of the world. The aim of the enemy was to destroy this people of God; he kept on stirring up the hatred of various nations in order to annihilate Israel. This attempt at annihilation becomes particularly conspicuous at three points in the history recorded in the Scriptures.

The first attempt occurred as soon as the descendants of Jacob had grown into a people in Egypt. The blessing on Abraham had passed through Isaac and Jacob to their many descendants. This was sufficient to stir the enemy to action. Hard oppressions and pitiless forced labor were systematically applied to wear the people down, but since they only increased in numbers, Pharaoh commanded that every newborn boy be killed at once. But how did the Lord react? He brought His people out of Egyptian bondage with a high hand, amid signs and miracles. And who became the leader of His people? Moses, who in his infancy was one of the little Jewish children who were to be killed immediately after their birth. We remember how his mother defied Pharaoh's command and hid little

Moses in a basket in the reeds of the Nile. Who can hinder the mighty God when He wants to rescue? All attempts to destroy God's loving plan for the world were (and still are) transformed by the Lord Himself into a triumph of His power and glory.

Another attack of the enemy followed about a thousand years later. The kingdom had been divided. Ten tribes had fallen away from the Davidic dynasty, subsequently to go into Assyrian exile. Only Judah and Benjamin, with Levi, remained as special bearers of the promise of the coming Saviour; they remained specially visible on the stage of the world. But about one hundred and fifty years later Judah was also forced into exile in Babylon. When Darius the Mede conquered Babylon, a small number of Jews returned to Jerusalem. Most of them remained, and were scattered throughout the 127 provinces of the Persian empire. Once again we find ourselves at a moment of crisis in the history of salvation.

Just at this time, when the people of God were living among Gentiles as tolerated aliens, far away from the land of their fathers and from Jerusalem, the city of their God, there came the next great attack of the tempter. This time the people were to be exterminated, not by a slow process, but abruptly and without exception. All were to be murdered, young and old, the babe and the grey-haried together. This story is to be found in the book of Esther. The burning hatred of one man produced a sentence of death for all Jews, a sentence which could not be countermanded. Haman had immense influence with the Persian king, and he devised a very clever scheme. Even the day of the pogrom was fixed. From the human point of view there was not the least hope of rescue.

But God—who or what can hinder Him? Even a situation which was so utterly hopeless could not hold up His plan to bring salvation to the world. It is wonderful to see how God availed Himself of somebody, also under the sentence of death, as an instrument of His rescue operation. It was the queen, Esther, herself a Jewess. Through her, the Lord turned all the evil meant for His people upon their enemies who sought their death. Thus the Lord manifested Himself both as judge against His enemies and as Saviour for His people. No wonder that many Medes and Persians, seeing such an obvious glorification of the Lord, desired to belong to such a wonderful God and became themselves Jews, as it is reported in the Bible (Esther 8:17).

We must see clearly that the first of the two attempts at annihilation we have just mentioned was aimed at Israel as a whole, and the second at Judah. We see the circle being drawn closer, until the attack was made on One alone, the One promised to Judah: Jesus. It was because of this child that Herod, driven by fear and jealousy, ordered the killing of all the boys of two and under in Bethlehem and the region round about. He wanted to be sure that the new-born King should not grow up, but should be exterminated. We know how God intervened and commanded Joseph to flee with Mary and the child to Egypt.

We must look back once again, so as to grasp something of immense importance. When the enemy attempted to destroy the work of God, he always tried to kill, annihilate, blot out. His goal was nothing less than the final solution of the Jewish problem. The child Jesus was also included in Satan's plan of annihilation. But when we come to the story of the temptation, where the enemy stands face to face with the One from the house of Judah, with Jesus, we find that he turns all his cleverness and deceit toward achieving the exact opposite, that is, that Jesus *should not die*. How are we to account for such a surprising change of tactics? Jesus should not die, but live! Something quite decisive must have happened. What was it?

In fact something quite decisive had happened. Immediately before Jesus was led by the Spirit into the wilderness, He had had Himself baptized by John in the river Jordan. John called the people to repentance, and all Jerusalem and Judeah had come down to the river Jordan where they confessed their sins and were baptized. Jesus too, though He was without sin, asked for baptism and so identified Himself with sinners. By His baptism Jesus fully entered the road of salvation; He made the decisive step toward the cross. He took the sins of the world on Himself; the witness from heaven was, "This is my beloved Son, with whom I am well pleased." Jesus had come into the world with the mission from the Father to lay down His life. After the resurrection, Peter expressed it this way, "He Himself bore our sins in His body on the tree. . . ." And John, pointing at Jesus, said these prophetic words, "Behold the Lamb of God, who takes away the sin of the world." Hence there is a vital link between baptism and the cross; this is why the tempter confronted Jesus so soon. By His baptism Jesus placed Himself in the chain of promises, and thus provoked the Satanic attack, which from the very beginning was directed against the fulfillment of the promises of God. Only from the perspective of Golgotha can we rightly understand the story of the temptation; but it works the other way round as well: the story of the temptation throws light on the tremendous event at Golgotha, which moved heaven and earth. If we separate the cross of Jesus from His temptation by the enemy, we ourselves fall victim to the tempter's ruse, and instead of seeing the victory of God's love for the whole world, we are misled to see in the crucifixion a sign of guilt, forgetting that on the contrary His death on the cross was Christ's act of reconciliation which is valid forever—for Israel and for the whole world. If we proclaim a gospel from which the Jew is excluded, we leave the foundation of the Scriptures and will be preaching a gospel that ceases to be the power of God even for the Gentiles.

No power could deter God from bringing salvation to the world through the atoning death of Jesus. All forces which oppose it are crushed on the rock of the unfailing faithfulness and steadfast love of God, the God of Israel. No force will ever prevent the triumphant march of God in which He will reveal His full glory to all nations. Because Jesus *will* come again! He will come in obvious power and glory as foretold by the prophets. The way that is marked by God's love goes on uninterrupted toward its God-appointed goal. The bearers of these promises are still the very same people: Israel. For this reason alone, the enemy never ceased to attack them again and again. Even in our time we saw the terrible attack against God's people through Hitler. And how did the Lord react? By reestablishing the State of Israel, where we can see His blessing upon the land. God wonderfully preserves His people to glorify Himself through them at His return.

But before Israel as a whole will experience this fullness of grace, the gathering of the Ecclesia must take place; it has been proceeding ever since Pentecost. The Ecclesia, the body of Christ as Paul calls it, consists of both Jews and Gentiles. They are the firstfruits, the witnesses on this earth of the finished work of salvation on Calvary and the coming of the new creation. For if anyone is in Christ, he is a new creation.

The Church is today the light in this world's darkness. Hence it is, just like Israel, exposed to the attacks of the enemy who wants to extinguish this light. By His attitude in temptation Jesus showed us clearly how we should tackle a crisis and face the enemy. He defeated every attack by using the sword of the Word of God.

He answered the tempter, "It is written . . . ." The risen Christ placed the same weapon in the hands of His disciples, and through them it has come down to us: the whole of the Holy Scriptures, the prophetic Word. Peter said, "And we have the prophetic word made more sure; you will do well to pay attention to this as to a light shining in a dark place, until the day dawns and the morning star rises in your hearts." The darker this world becomes, the more false doctrines and lies slip into the church—thus confusing and deceiving many. Only when we stand on the rock of the *whole* of the Scriptures, draw our life from it, and defend ourselves with it, can we win victory through Jesus, the Victor. Amen.

Chapter 8

# The New Song

*I waited patiently for the Lord; he inclined to me and heard my cry. He drew me up from the desolate pit, out of the miry bog. And he set my feet upon a rock, making my steps secure. He put a new song in my mouth, a song of praise to our God...* (Psalm 40:1–3).

IN THESE FEW VERSES OF PSALM 40 we read how the Lord put a new song in David's mouth. But this can and ought to happen to us all. Our cry, whether it be a cry for help or a cry of repentance, can be transformed into a wonderful new song. To understand how this miraculous change can take place, let us be led by David to the very place where he had this wonderful experience.

We see David for the first time as the youngest son of Jesse in Bethlehem. But he was not merely the youngest son; in his father's eyes he was the most insignificant. When the Lord sent His prophet Samuel to Jesse's house to anoint one of his sons to be king over Israel, David did not even come into consideration. And yet it was this very David whom God chose to be king over His people Israel.

It must have been an overwhelming surprise to him to be called from the sheep—called from the pasture to be lifted up to such a high position: king, *king over the people of God.* Many beautiful psalms echo the love and joy of his heart; but even upon the occasion of such an event we do not hear the "new song" bursting from his lips.

Later we see David as a hero, the victor over Goliath. David loved his God, just as the Lord expressed love in His own words: " . . . with all [his] heart, with all [his] soul, with all [his] might." And here we have the secret of a victorious life with God. It was this love for his God that made it impossible for him to endure the continuing slander of the giant and his defiance of the army of the living God. So in his love for God and with living faith he entered the unequal fight with the armored Goliath.

Do not think for a moment that David was a dreamer; he was a very sober young man. He was fully aware of the strength of the armored giant and of his own bodily weakness compared to the giant; but David was a man who looked up to his God. We are shown clearly and plainly what living faith looks like. Faith means to count on the living God, on His presence, His promises, His power, His wisdom, His love. We also rejoice and gain new courage to trust in God through the wonderful victory the Lord gave him over Goliath. Why has it been recorded by the Holy Spirit in the Bible? That we who live after the great victory of the Son of David on the cross of Calvary over the eternal enemy, the real Goliath, may be remided how to take up the fight with our respective giants. Yes, we Christians have our own "Goliaths" who defy us again and again, and like David we are challenged to prove our faith and courage to take up the fight in the name of Him who has already won the victory: Jesus. Do not forget: when you are facing a situation, a temptation, which seems to be far beyond your strength, you must not lose faith. Look up to Jesus the Victor, and in His name dare to take up the fight. He will glorify Himself through your trust, your faith. Mind you, the

## The New Song / 107

victory might be in one of two ways: either that your "Goliath" has to flee, or that you receive the strength and the peace to endure the trial in a way that makes you a real testimony to others, and brings you out of the test richer, riper, and with a faith tried in the fire.

We can be sure that David was deeply impressed and overwhelmed by the victory granted to him over Goliath. Even so the "new song" did not spring from this glorious occasion either.

Later we see David on the road of tribulation. Though he was anointed to be king, Saul was still on the throne, and persecuted David with a jealous hatred. Often David was in real danger, and on many occasions it was only the Lord's wonderful intervention that saved his life.

During the time of persecution in Hungary I learned what danger of death means. I learned what it feels like to go about with the yellow star of David sewn to my clothes—to be like a sheep on the way to be slaughtered. But it was just at that time of horror that I experienced the comforting presence of the Lord, in the midst of the raging enemies of God. He gave to those who were destined to die a most wonderful peace and strength to take into death. Others He rescued, such as myself, and we are meant to speak of His faithfulness in standing by us. At that time I learned that the persecution of the Jews is the proof of the hatred of the enemies of God against the witnesses of His reality. That is why not only Jews were a target of that hatred and in danger of their lives, but committed Christians as well.

So many of David's psalms were a source of comfort to us in the dark hours we had to go through, for he sings praises to the Lord as the Good Shepherd who neither slumbers nor sleeps. And the 124th Psalm, where David invites Israel to praise God for His faithfulness! He says, "If it had not been the Lord who was on our side, when men rose up against us, they would have swallowed us up alive when their anger was kindled against us . . . Blessed be the Lord, who has not given us a prey to their teeth . . . Our help is in the name of the Lord. . . ." What wonderful psalms—but such wonderful experiences notwithstanding, we still do not hear the "new song."

Finally, we see David as the greatest king of Israel. No other was elevated so high as he. Remember, David received the Lord's promise that the eternal King whose reign will never end, the Messiah, will be an earthly offspring of his. How enthusiastically David praises the Lord for this great honor. He is amazed, he worships, he adores. But he is still not jubilating the "new song," even at this peak of his life.

If this were all, and only the heights of David's life had been recorded for us, the 3,000-year-old story would not have much relevance for us today. We might admire David, we might find his life fascinating, but what else would he have to say to us who live today? Nothing at all.

But thank God there is something else recorded about David, something that historians would have politely and tactfully ignored and concealed. There is a stain, a disgrace, in his life. We are shown a sin in David's life by which it is demonstrated to us that even the mightiest king of Israel was a fallible sinner. As Paul put it, "None is righteous, no, not one"—not even the greatest king of Israel. The man whom God chose as a man according to His own heart was unmasked as a sinner.

Now we find David at the very spot mentioned in Psalm 40, in the desolate pit, in the miry bog of the sin he has committed with Bathsheba. And we see, as he tries to save himself by his own efforts, how he sinks even deeper, committing an even greater sin—a perfidious murder. But overwhelmed and convicted by the prophet Nathan, David declares himself guilty. Then he cries to God—to God who is his only hope and refuge. In Psalm 51 we hear his cry of repentance out of the depth, out of the miry bog: "Have mercy upon me, O God, according to thy love, and blot out my transgression . . . wash me and I shall be whiter than snow. . . ." But this time he cries to God as to his *Saviour.* It is wonderful to see in so many places in the Old Testament how the Lord speaks to His people and says, "I am your God, your Saviour." Saviour, Yeshua, Jesus. David cries to his Saviour as his only hope.

And here we see the greatest miracle that has ever happened on this earth, the greatest that can happen at all. How eager we are to experience a miracle! Here is one, the greatest of all, in which the holy God (as it is written in Isaiah 57 "who is dwelling in the high and holy places") hears the cry of a sinner who calls for help. He also hears your call. He is the same today. The Lord hears it and inclines to the deepest depth of the desolate pit to meet a sinner who cries to Him, who calls for deliverance. The Lord seizes David by the hands, lifts him up from the pit, and places his feet on a rock. The expression of joy over such a deliverance and salvation—that, my friends, is the "new song." No one has ever tasted real joy who has not experienced this deep joy of deliverance. And the rock upon which the Lord placed David's feet is none but Himself—the eternal God who in the person of Jesus became our Saviour, our Rock, yesterday, today, and forever the same.

At this point I invite you to come and wonder with me. It is such a pity that Christians fail to wonder and be amazed at the loving thoughts of the Lord which are also recorded in the Old Testament. That is why the gospel of Christ which Paul preached as the power of

*110* / The Eternal Covenant

God for salvation begins with Genesis. Paul and all the other apostles who led thousands of Jews and Gentiles to the risen Lord said so. The whole of the Scriptures is the gospel.

Isn't it wonderful to see that a thousand years before Jesus the Lamb of God came to take away the sin of the world, David has such certainty that his sins were forgiven? Think of Psalm 103 where David sings praises to God for the forgiveness of all his sins. Isn't it wonderful! If we Christians living after the finished work of redemption on Calvary have this wonderful assurance, that is natural. But David, and all the pious of Israel before Calvary—how could they have such assurance? It is written that "without shedding of blood there is no remission of sins." That is why God Himself gave the blood of atonement upon the altar for His people Israel. In Leviticus 17:11 we read, "For the life of the flesh is in the blood, and I [God] have given it for you upon the altar to make an atonement for your souls. . . ." Israel at all times lived by the forgiving grace of the Lord. Every year the Lord reconciled the whole people of Israel on the day of atonement through the blood of the sacrificed animals. The high priest brought the sacrifice for his own sins, and then he entered the holy of holies to present the blood of atonement upon the golden plate of the ark of the covenant. The writer of the Epistle to the Hebrews reminds all Hebrews who knew of that atonement through the blood of the animals how Christ appeared as a high priest—and He entered once and for all into the holy place taking, not the blood of goats and calves, but His own blood, thus securing eternal redemption. That is why the blood of Jesus is the blood of reconciliation for Israel, and for the whole world.

Let us go back to David again. We see that he had good reason to sing the "new song" with joy and praise.

One more question arises: How did David recognize that he had sinned against God and that he needed forgiveness? I will make the question quite personal: How do we come to see that we need forgiveness, that we really need a Saviour? What is it that urges us to cry to God as to our Saviour and then experience and taste the joy of forgiveness? Paul gives the answer: "Through the law comes the knowledge of sin" (Rom. 3:30). In other words, through the ten commandments. David too was led to repentance through the knowledge of the Law. So he knew that what he had done could not stand before God. It is wonderful to see that the Lord never used the deeds of the law to bring anybody out of the miry pit of sin. David was also rescued, not by the deeds of the law, but through the forgiveness and grace of God. The Law is like a mirror. But the Lord does not use the mirror to wash us clean; that is done by the blood of atonement.

Finally, the verses we read in Psalm 40 do not just describe the experiences of millions of Jews and Christians; they are also messianic. They are prophetic words that have since been fulfilled. A thousand years after David, the promised Seed of David was born. The little Jewish babe born to the virgin Mary of the house of David was the promised King. But in a most wonderful way He did not come to reign as an ordinary king. He came to serve and to lay down His life as a ransom. That is why He became man. In Hebrews 2:14 we read, "Since the children share in flesh and blood, He [Jesus] himself partook of the same nature, that through death he might destroy him who had the power of death, that is, the devil." Jesus became man to take up the fight with the real Goliath, and to bring an eternal and final victory. That is why He, to whom all honor and praise is due, humbled Himself, being born in the likeness of man—humbled Himself, being obedient unto death, even death on the cross. Jesus became the Lamb of God to take away the sin of the world. God laid upon Him the sin of us all, and with the sin of the world upon His body He went into the deepest depth, into the miry bog; and on Good Friday, from the cross, we hear a cry. When Jesus, who was made sin for us, cried "My God, my God, why have you forsaken me?" the holy God, the Father, inclined to the depth of hell and lifted up the obedient Servant and highly exalted Him, bestowing on Him the highest name in heaven or on earth. Jesus was lifted up through the resurrection. Since that victory we have a new and living way through His blood. He is our Psalm of praise, our Rock of salvation, and the source of eternal joy. To His praise we shall sing "a new song." Amen.

A true story from Werfel: *Stories from Two Worlds*

A rabbi was talking to a Roman Catholic priest. He said: "I do not know, sir, why the Church is so concerned with baptizing the Jews. Is it satisfied by winning perhaps two or three real believers among a hundred renegades, moved by worldly ambitions or weakness? In any case, what would happen if all Jews in the world were baptized?—Israel would disappear. With its disappearance the single real physical witness to Divine revelation would vanish from the world. The Holy Scriptures both of the Old and the New Testaments would sink then to the level of an empty and powerless mythology like the myths of ancient Egypt and Greece. Does the Church not recognize this deadly danger? It is particularly deadly at a time when everything is in a state of flux. We belong together, sir, but we are not a unity. As you know better than I, we are told in Romans that the community of the Messiah is based on Israel. I am convinced that Israel will last as long as the Church, and also that if Israel falls the Church will also. . . ."

"What led you to this conviction?" asked the priest.

"Our sufferings down to the present day," answered the rabbi. "Do you really think that God would have endured us and kept us for centuries without any real purpose?"